Names Without Tombs
A Personal Memoir of Salonika, Greece
1917-1943

Semaya Abraham Levy
with William A. Meis, Jr.

Published December 15, 2016
Fallen Bros. Press
Rancho Palos Verdes CA 90275

ISBN-10:0-9976728-2-X
ISBN-13:978-0-9976728-2-4

Translations from the original Ladino & Greek:
Bryan Kirschen
Natasha Pavlidou

Cover and interior design: © Guillermo Bosch, 2016

Front Cover Art: © Amy Labagh

Financial support for this project was provided by:
The Estate of Elvira Levy

Dedication:

To the 25 million innocent souls.
To the 6.5 million innocent Jews.
To my dear father, mother, brother, sister, and Gracia.
To the many American, English, French, Russian and
other soldiers who found death as the cost of liberation.
May all their souls rest in peace. Amen.

Contents   Page

Salonika, view outside the ancient wall guarding the old city, circa 1895.

Salonika, the White Tower, view from the sea, circa 1800.

Prologue: 1492
No ay mas sodro de aquel ke non kiere oyir.
(There is no one more deaf than he who does not want to hear.)
-Sephardic Proverb

Where else in all of the Old World before the end of Empires, were Jews in such glory as those in Thessaloniki, the forgotten Jews of Thessaloniki, the Ladino Jews, the Sephardic Jews, exiled from Spain in 1492, yes, that same year the Italian mariner, Cristoforo Colombo was forced to embark for the New World—America, from the small port of Palos de la Frontera, because that same Spanish Queen, Isabella, who sent Colombo also announced "The Alhambra Decree," clogging the larger ports of Spain with 200,000 Jews, stripped of their homes and heritage, their synagogues topped by crosses, wailing into the night, knowing tombs of their ancestors were abandoned to dust, shocked to find themselves Wandering Jews, alone, barely escaping the fires of the Inquisition, the ovens of the Dominicans.

Set adrift on the warm waters of the Mediterranean Sea, they stumbled into North Africa, tumbled into Arabia, fumbled their way along the coast of Anatolia, but a good number, a very good number indeed, found themselves settled in Greece, in the glorious city of Thessaloniki, named, in truly ancient times for Princess Thessalonike of Macedon, half sister to Alexander the Great, this thriving merchant city, crown Jewel of Byzantium, then diamond to the Ottomans, capital of the Sanjak of Selanik, became a sanctuary—heart of Ladino power, that rarest of places before *Eretz*

Israel, where Jews could be rich-or-poor, ruler-or-ruled, boss-or-worker, all professions, all stations open to them for they were not the "them" but the "they" who held sway over Greeks, Armenians, Turks, Albanians, Roma and Bulgarians, in Thessaloniki—Salonika to Ladino Jews, sometimes *A Madre de Israel* (Mother of Israel), City of The White Tower, the Jews of Salonika dominating trade throughout the Eastern Mediterranean, spinning wool into Salonika blankets, sheets and carpets with inherited Iberian skills for the rich in Smyrna, Alexandria, and Istanbul. Bathing in the Yehudi Hamam, their cortijos (courtyards) ripe with figs, pomegranates and lemons, their jujube trees gave shade from the hot summer sun and the scents of jasmine and roses perfumed their homes.

Salonika Jewish woman in traditional dress, circa 1913.

So they were not watching, they were not listening, they were unprepared for the flames that engulfed the city, for the flames that burned from resentment in the humiliations of Macedonia and Thrace, for the flames of those distant ovens waiting for the trains rolling north toward Auschwitz-Birkenau and Mauthausen, their centuries-old escape from Tomás de Torquemada becoming God's cruel joke that took 500 years to reach its bitter punch line.

We will weep at the end of this sad tale for the Lost Jews of Salonika, for the Names Without Tombs, for the bodies of those who once walked in the sunlight, becoming ashes, smoke-scattered by frigid winds across unkind Northern European forests. But do not weep at the beginning, as I, Semaya Abraham Levy, take pen in hand to bear witness that there remain stories and songs that still resonate inside my personal kabbalah of the time when we lived before death, when gentler flames gave warmth, happiness and sustenance for celebration and for joy…

*****

The Rabbi and the Inquisitor
(A Sephardic Story)

The City of Seville in Spain was seething with foreboding. A Christian boy had been found dead, and the Jews were falsely accused by their enemies of having murdered him in order to use his blood for ritual in the baking of matzos for Passover. So the Rabbi was brought before the Grand Inquisitor to stand trial as Leader of the Jewish Community.

The Grand Inquisitor hated the Rabbi, but despite all his efforts to prove that the crime had been committed by the Jews, the Rabbi succeeded in disproving the charge. Seeing that he had been beaten in argument, the Inquisitor turned his eyes piously to Heaven and said, "We will leave the Judgment of this matter to God. Let there be a drawing of lots. I shall deposit two pieces of paper in a box. On one I shall write the word guilty, the other will have no writing on it. If the Jew draws the first, it will be a sign from Heaven that the Jews are guilty, and we'll have him burned at the stake. If he draws the second, on which there is no writing, it will be divine proof of the Jew's innocence, so we'll let him go".

Now the Grand Inquisitor was a cunning fellow. He was anxious to burn the Jew and since he knew that no one would ever find out about it, he decided to write the word "guilty" on both pieces of paper.

The Rabbi suspected he was going to do just this, therefore, when he put his hand into the box and drew forth a piece of paper he quickly put it into his mouth and swallowed it.

"What is the meaning of this, Jew?" raged the Inquisitor. "How do you expect us to know which paper you drew now that you've swallowed it?"

"Very simple" replied the Rabbi, "you have only to look at the paper that remains in the box."

3

So they took out the piece of paper still in the box. "There!" cried the Rabbi triumphantly. "This paper says guilty, therefore the one I swallowed must have been blank. Now, you must release me!"

*****

Estherinica
by S. Saby
(A Sephardic song that in the original Ladino plays on the repetitions and the rhythms of the words)

My little sister,
Born in a little blanket
Round, round,
Like the base of a wave
A wave of milk,

The fish is arriving
Fish in the rain
Out comes a bucket
A bucket, my lady.
At the Northern Gate of Thessaloniki

There is a crowd of little hens
Singing "kukurikoo"

Open the box,
Silver and gold
Open the suitcase,
Liras and gold
Under the ladder,
A small pot
So full of blood and substance
Whoever speaks, will drink from it.

Salonika salep vendors, circa 1914

The Vendor of Salep

(From the pen of Joseph Covo, may his soul rest in peace, an historian and man of letters who died in Salonika in 1942, from hunger during the German occupation, and just before the deportation of Salonika's Jews from the city by the Germans.)

Who is this, who sings in his sweet and harmonious voice in the loneliness of the night when all are at rest and dreaming, in order to praise his wares, and who gets the neighborhoods so excited that everyone longs to hear his song?

It is the salep [a milk and flower based hot drink made from the dried powdered roots of a mountain orchid] vendor who circles the streets, and sings the ballads that he learned from his grandparents:

Tonight gentlemen.
I will sleep with a lady;
In all my days,
I have not found one quite like her.
   He cries out:
Salep, salep!
Hot, Hot!
   Little Samuel the vendor of salep, continues his romantic old Sephardic ballad:

5

She was white and red,
Red-headed like a candle.

At the slope of a river
And the peaks of a valley
I met Meliselda...
Milk salep!
Hot salep!

The ladies and gentlemen call little Samuel, Samuelico, the vendor of salep.
The ladies are ready, ready!

And more and more romantically, he continues:
I met with Meliselda
The daughter of the ruling class
Who came from the baths,
From the cold baths
To wash herself and get dressed...
Salep, salep!

But before serving the ladies, they ask for the end of the ballad.

Samuelico serves his milk salep, or the salep full of cinnamon that all the Sephardim adore. And, while young men and women taste his salep, they call into the air sweet notes, sharp and melancholic, "Encore! Encore!" They cry from all directions, but Samuelico has other concerns. He is a bit like Don Quixote—at times a grasshopper but also an ant.

Life is life, and you have to count on it. Don't you see the temperament of our tribe? Ballad and salep, ideal and spiritually practical.
Salep, salep! Hot salep!

And then Samuelico announces himself in other neighborhoods, to the words of other ballads. For he knows how to sing at dawn. And Samuelico, the street psychologist, who knows the likes of his compatriots, satisfies his clients, with one of the best ballads of the repertoire; one of the ballads where the music and the melody have the gift of moving even the most hardhearted.
Tomorrow, tomorrow,
there's only tomorrow;

When it wants to leave,
The daily star.

This ballad, so loved by all of the Sephardim, is Samuelico's triumph. So Samuelico sings, proclaims, and announces his milk salep. And in the silence of the night, Samuelico readies himself before going to the ladies, to the young ladies, who pay attention to the last part of his song:

Lady, my lady
Who keeps us alive?
The book and the rose
And the grain of wheat,
And a pretty lady
that with me may sleep.

"Encore! Encore!" Again, laughs and happiness. "Encore! Encore!" But Samuelico goes around the plaza announcing his salep, and the thin refrain of his songs arrives to just so many ears before his silhouette disappears little by little, and is then lost in the darkness of the night.

True dawn is about to appear. The first rooster crows; the neighborhood light changes from the clear moon to the sun. Silence reigns; it is finally dawn. But then the silence is disturbed by the shouts of the shamash [caretaker of the synagogue], who invites the observant ones to prayer in the morning, "To Prayer! To prayer! For you must get up to make the minyan! To prayer!"

*****

The Fair Lady
(A Sephardic ballad brought from Spain)

The fair lady was washing,
Washing and spreading out her clothes.
With tears she washed,
With sighs that filled her.

A knight came by

And asked for a cup of water from her.
With tears from her eyes,
She filled seven jugs for him.

Why do you cry, fair lady?
Why do you cry?

Everyone is returning from the war
And my husband has not returned.

Tell me how to spot him, my lady
And I will look for him.

Tall, tall like a pine tree,
Straight like an arrow.
He has a blonde beard,
Beginning to appear on him.

I saw him, my lady.
He was killed in the war,
Two wounds from a sword
Stained the collar of his jacket.

He said three things to me
An hour before he died:
"I have a beautiful wife."
"You should marry her."

I will not marry anyone.
I have waited for him for seven years
And I will wait another seven.
And if in the eighth
He does not come,
I shall remain a widow.

And the third thing that he said to me was
"On her right breast, she has a birthmark."

Lift your arm, for I see
You have a large birthmark.

Upon hearing these words, she
Lay down on top of him and kissed him.

*****

...Ah! These stories and songs of love, and romance, of the warm lives of the Ladino of Salonika, the Lost Jews of Salonika, of the Names Without Tombs.

And in those earlier days, when Salonika was still governed by the Ottomans, before our modern steel machines began to mindlessly manufacture identical perfection unimaginable even in dreams, there were dozens of beneficent ovens in Salonika, ovens made for baking not for burning, the ovens like those used to make matzah for the days of Passover.

The most renowned of those were the ovens of Salomon Koen, Mair Gerchon, and Uziel's widow, may their names be remembered, all known for "water matzah". And let us not forget Perahia's oven and the "wine matzah" the taste of which lingers on in the memory of this old Salonika Jew.

With the approaching of Tu-Bishvat, the owners of those ovens prepared them, whitewashed them, cleaned them, steamed them, and to do these jobs, they employed Jewish nieces, daughters, cousins who, during their work, continuously sang the Spanish ballads of love and loss, of passion and release, of dreams and fantasies.

Remember now, young Esmeralda, the daughter of Haskia el Garonudo, who was beautiful, so beautiful she burned hearts and with her lovely voice sang siren songs that made the young men crazy for her—slack-jawed when they heard her sing "The Star of Diana" which, if memory serves, began:

Early in the morning
So early in the morning
When the star of Diana

Desired to appear,

I set forth on a journey,
And I went to Yanina
To see if I could find her,
My pretty lady.

In the midst of the journey
There I found her.

Lady, my lady.
With dark beauty marks
Remove the dark ones
And put on your wings…

Since the matzah ovens were never turned off (do not think ahead, nor let your mind wander to future ovens that burned day and night or you will spoil the memory of matzah), they baked 24 hours a day, and many young men would show up to see their lovers or fiancés, but the bosses would not permit the young women to come and go. The injustice of that! And so, many problems arose (and truth be told, some disputes ended at the police station) because the bosses and their associates often abused their advantage with the beautiful young workers and the young men were not happy.

Even so, it was often noted that poor girls working the ovens were sometimes seen as achieving "great success" in becoming the wife of a rich man that fell in love with the young girl's beauty or her haunting voice.…

*****

El Nora Alila
by Haim Chalem

In the great community of Salonika, very conservative in past times, a very interesting event happened at the sacred moment of the prayer "El Nora Alila" on the evening of Yom Kippur. My father, of blessed memory, told me what happened, and I want to tell it so it is known to everyone because it is good to remember past events that teach us of the paths that our grandfathers took so as to correct their children.

Fifty years ago, there lived a good Jew, fearful of God with all his soul. As was the tradition then, he would not miss any prayer, and he was a truly religious kind of man for he would always engage in the Torah and was honest in business. He had great success and in very little time he became one of the great men of the city. He was very rich, very wise, and very honored. He lacked just one thing: children. But eventually he also managed to have one son.

Everything was done so that this son would be deserving of such a father. A good school, private teachers, esteemed educators. In a word, everything was provided so that the son would receive the necessary tools for the battle that is life. Unfortunately, the heavens did not help, and the son ended up being the very worst. He had many faults, and his good father was faced with hardship and misfortune. All of the father's efforts to set the son on a good path were useless: the son undid the father's success from left to right, without ever thinking of the consequences.

Time passed and the father realized that his time had arrived to leave this world. He called his only son to say goodbye to him and then to die in peace. On some occasions, this scene can be very moving—an agonizing father speaking to his son who only caused him misfortune in life.

"Listen to me at this time, my son," said the father. "I beg you to turn to a straight path so that you may enjoy all of the property that I am leaving you. Don't continue on this road, because this will lead you to misery and dishonor. I am convinced that your life will end very badly if you do not change your ways. In any case, I want you to promise me in this moment, on my deathbed, that whatever may happen, you will not sell the three prayer books that I leave you. That of Rosh Hashanah, that of Yom Kippur, and that of Sukkot."

The son was very touched and promised his father he would do so, and the father gave his soul to God while hugging his son. The father went to Heaven and the upset son remained in the Hell below, a sold slave to his vices.

A little time passed by with him dragging along, poor, circling the taverns and often needing of a piece of bread, but always carrying the three books that he promised not to sell. He took them everywhere he went, and even in the most serious moments did not think of selling them. For him, the three books were all that remained of the father who complained of his conduct and whose spirit followed him day and night. The son often went without eating for days, unknown and far from everyone. He slept underneath the stairs having beneath his head just those sacred and legendary books.

One day on the streets he heard that it was the evening of Yom Kippur, and one would need to fast early and go to the synagogue for prayer. A flash of light shined in the eyes of the unfortunate son, and he decided to spend the day of Yom Kippur in the synagogue. That being said, he took the book on Yom Kippur, and without even fasting, he went to one of the synagogues.

Upon entering, many knew him and remembered his unlucky father. In a corner, alone, he started to pray with everyone, but in a very low voice because he was very ashamed for having fallen so low. On Yom Kippur evening, he asked the shamash for permission to spend the night on one of the benches in the synagogue, being that he had no where to sleep. In the morning they entered into prayer again until the time arrived for the closing prayer, which was called "El Nora Alila."

The son, who was calm until this time, praying in a low voice, started to let out fearsome cries. He sung the "El Nora Alila" prayer more loudly than anyone else.

Once the prayers were finished and everyone prepared to break the fast, the cantor, an old friend of his father, approached him to know the reason for his shouting. "What happened to you, my son," he asked. "Why were you screaming so much? Do you not feel well?"

The son, repenting and crying from happiness, responded to the cantor, "No, sir. I am very well, better than ever. I have now turned to the righteous path that my father wanted so badly. God answered me on this Yom Kippur." He showed the cantor a note that his father had attached to the page of the "El Nora Alila" prayer, worth 10 thousand golden liras.

From that moment he became a man of good fortune, straightforward and honest, just as his father had wished for him to be.

*****

...And so we lived our comfortable lives, our beautiful lives, with stories and songs and legends brought from Spain and handed down generation after generation through my family and all the families of Salonika, when talk of fires and flames revealed our passions, our guilt, our lusts, our warmth, our love and our generous, joyous Sephardic blood.

But yes, it is true we were not watching, we were not listening, we were unprepared for those first flames that engulfed the city striking a staggering blow from which we were never to recover—an omen of what was to come, a warning, (from God? Perhaps...) but still, we would not listen.

(l. to r.) Semaya Abraham Levy in 1916, with his grandfather, Semaya, and cousin, Avram.

Chapter 1: The Great Fire of Salonika
La notche esta saga, el dia mira detras.
(The night is slow, and the day watches carefully from behind.)
-Sephardic Proverb

Shabbat afternoon at 2 o'clock
Fire came out from New Water…

This was the song that rose from the throats of the Sephardic people, from each wretched family, from every Jewish child whose life was changed by this fire that did us such great harm, and burned so destructively in the Jewish quarters of Salonika.

It was on Shabbat Day, August 17, 1917, when a homeless, perhaps disturbed, Greek lady, who lived at Olympiados #3, in the higher elevations of the city, the less desirable areas of the city, in the district then called "New Water," and also "Mevlane," wanted to make a delicious meal from the eggplants she had brought from the marketplace. She filled her little stove with wood, too much wood, and began to fry the eggplants in olive oil, too much olive oil. In a distracted moment, a careless moment, the woman allowed the oil to jump from the skillet and land on the fire. Sparks from the fire jumped onto the walls of her little hovel constructed from reeds and thin sticks, and the fire then jumped from her tiny hut to the surrounding houses, and soon began to spread even further due to a powerful wind, and in a matter of minutes, the entire New Water district was engulfed in flames, and then from New Water the fire jumped and tumbled down out of the hillsides to the Ministry building on the Agiou Dimitriou road, and to the market via the Leontos Sofou road, into the central districts of Salonika, the port districts, the Jewish districts where it became a massive conflagration that overcame the meager fire hydrants and the pitiful lack of available water.

As the fierce winds blew, the fire consumed Jewish businesses, Jewish synagogues, the Post Office, the telegraph office, the water company's headquarters, the gas company's headquarters, the Ottoman Bank, the National Bank of Greece, the Bank of Athens, and the seat of the chief rabbi with all its archives, Jewish homes—their courtyards, their fig, pomegranate and lemon trees, their jujube trees, their jasmine and their roses. All gone. Everything leveled to the ground.

*****

The Grinder
(A Sephardic Poem)

I grind and I grind
Water in the mortar.
No one takes pity on
This foreigner.
Reaching you is such a hard thing,
For he who wants to die, regrets it.

Enough speaking, lad, you don't get tired
Of this chatter; you are not fooling me
In telling me so.

I am tired
From your fire, and I have already roasted
If you roasted too, you can just say it.
For mine is worse as it remains covered.

Come hear what the world has to offer
I will recite 30 coplas for you in a minute

Enough worrying, lad
At the end of the year, be sure not to catch tuberculosis,
[May you have] strong beginnings and good endings.

*****

It was so, so long ago, so many, many tragedies ago, and I was so little then that I can only barely remember what the great fire was like, but there are terrible visions that I cannot forget of the sparkling embers raining down from the skies falling upon our heads, and the explosions that sent huge plumes of smoke and flames into the sky.

As in all such tragedies, the people, especially the older people sought reasons for the tragedy, sought explanations that would allow them to understand their misfortune, and so they gossiped and raged and ranted among themselves, inventing answers out of chaos. The especially religious proclaimed that it was the wrath of God visited upon the citizens of Salonika for the sins of the Sabbath, for continually violating the prohibitions of the Sabbath.

Others contended that it was the allied troops—the soldiers of the French and English and Serbian armies who were then stationed in Greece in order to fight the Central Powers, the Germans, the Austro-Hungarians and Bulgarians—and that it was those very allied troops who started the fire.

Others speculated about how it could be possible for a woman frying eggplant to cause such a conflagration and why she was cooking so carelessly at that time of day. And then there were those others who could not find a scapegoat for their suspicions, but they were certain it was not the Greek woman at Olympiados #3.

And so, as rumors spread and blame was demanded, it was the elders, with their superstitions and ancient fears, who prevailed with their explanation that it was punishment for the Sins of the Sabbath and it was their view that became the legend declared in the children's song:

Teaching little children

Devastated Salonika street after the fire, 1917.

the sins of the Sabbath,
The ruler of the world
became merciless and
sent us to Dudular and Kara-Isin…

Now Dudular, Camp Campbell and Kara-Isin were neighborhoods five to seven kilometers from Thessaloniki proper, and also the areas where the foreign soldiers had placed their camps. To their credit, the soldiers did erect shelters and tent cities to house as many Jews as they could, but it was to their discredit that these same armies refused to provide us with water and assistance while the fire ravaged the city, and why the blame was partly laid at the doorstep of those troops who were then burdened with the task of housing us.

At the time that the great fire had already become a monstrous firestorm surging into the city from the heights above the town, my unfortunate grandfather, also named Semaya for I was named after him, a strong independent man, both spiritually and physically who fought to carve out a comfortable life for his family, a man who had become perhaps too comfortable with his life in the sunshine, his home by the sea, his lovely wife, his proud children and chattering grandchildren, this white-bearded, but still powerful old man was immediately besieged outside the door of his house as he himself was also preparing to flee the oncoming fire, besieged by threatening crowds who, as they fled their homes already lost to the flames, came to remonstrate against him, shouting his name and cursing him because they considered him responsible for the evil visited upon them, responsible because my grandfather was too liberal in his ways and did not keep the Sabbath, responsible because he was an easy target for their fears.

"Brothers," my old grandfather shouted, "in the middle of this terror you have come to me and blame me for our collective pain and sorrow? Look not to me but for the help of God to save us from the flames!"

Still they cursed and shouted and waved their fists into the smoke-filled air as burning embers fell into the street at their feet.

And my grandfather called to them, "Save yourselves and save your children. Tomorrow we can search for explanations." Then he held up his own arm so that all could see. "Look, my brothers, I carry the amulet that Rabbi Haim made." As if the amulet were proof of his religiosity.

But no one could make sense of his words or even their own words in all of the panic and confusion and screaming, so my grandfather lifted me onto his shoulder, grabbed a pestle, a chamber pot, an ewer, and we ran from the flames. The crowd refocused on the fire and the danger. We all ran together, and my grandfather and I were able to survive.

After we arrived in Kara-Isin, our family gathered together, and among the exhaustion and devastation, we still found time for joy that we had all survived, and even some humor as we counted our meager possessions. I heard my grandmother, Oro, speak to my grandfather as he presented her with the pestle, the chamber pot and the ewer he had carried with him. "And the jewels! Did you take the jewels, Semaya?"

He sadly shook his head to indicate he had not brought the jewels.

Grandfather then tipped the ewer and held out the amulet as it fell into his hand.

"Here is the golden amulet," said my grandfather. "It is this amulet that saved my soul. It is enough for us just to be alive! Let the devil take the jewels."

Later my grandfather told me that he himself, and not Rabbi Haim, crafted the amulet!

*****

The Weary Man and the Angel of Death
(A Sephardic Parable)

A man was carrying a heavy load of wood on his shoulders. When he grew weary he let the bundle down and cried bitterly "O Death, come and take me!"

Survivors of the the Great Fire, Salonika, 1917.

Immediately, the Angel of Death appeared and asked "Why do you call me?"

Frightened, the man answered, "Please help me put this load back on my shoulders".

*****

After two days of burning, the fire died out, but three quarters of the Sephardic population of Salonika, 52,000 Jews, were without shelter, 4,096 of the 7,695 shops within the city were destroyed, and 70% of the workforce was unemployed. Here is how the people of Salonika lamented in their songs:

She who fried the eggplants
Left us poor, so poor…

We may ask, we may speculate, we may even hypothesize, that had not that first Great Fire burned out the Jews from the heart of Salonika, had it not sent large numbers of them away from the city and scattered them wandering again to other refuge along the shores of the Mediterranean, had it not diminished the powers and the numbers of the Jews of Salonika, then could those future flames, those future ovens have been avoided? Would the Jews of Salonika have been strong enough, powerful enough to withstand the jaws of the beast?

We will never know the answer to that question because the answer cannot be known, but we do know that if the Great Fire was a warning, a harbinger designed by God for the Jews of Salonika, the signs were not heeded and the meaning was lost in fruitless squabbling over the importance of keeping the Sabbath.

Chapter 2: Passover (A Seder after the Great Fire)
El Papa que instoro la inquizition tuvo y su maldision.
(The Pope that initiated the Inquisition was accursed.)
-Sephardic Proverb

The following Spring, my father, Abraham, gathered the family together for the Passover Seder, and he said, "This has been spoken by our forefathers and by us: That not one alone has risen up to destroy us, but rather in each and every generation, many rise to destroy us. And the Holy One, blessed be he, rescues us from their hands."

And then Abraham said, "My children, and Rachel, the beloved companion of my life, I want us to pay particular attention to these words that we read on this night of Passover, because it might be that you do not know what being Jewish means, or what 'pogroms' mean, but in each and every generation we have had them.

"Where should we begin, with the Inquisition of Torquemada, may his name be cursed, as told in the history that has been repeated by the brotherhood and at times by all the people, in the futile hope that our ancestors might someday be avenged, and someday able to rescind the decree of the expulsion from Spain by a dull-witted king and a fanatic queen who might recant their error. But it was in vain that Don Isaac Abravanel, that incredibly rich and distinguished Iberian Jew and renowned Sephardic scholar who was then the financier to the Catholic Ferdinand and Isabella, a man who had spent a great deal of his personal fortune supporting the Spanish Monarchy in their wars against the Moors,

The Levy Family in 1926, (from left clockwise) Semaya, Abraham, Aaron, Sabetico, Djilda.

entreated them, offering them 600,000 crowns for the revocation of the Edict of Alhambra, asking if they could imagine what it means to take away a homeland, to take away a land where one grew up, where one was educated, and to be sent wandering on the high seas in sailing ships, that were at the mercy of the pirates, when, in the middle of his negotiations with the king and queen, the Grand Inquisitor Torquemada appeared and threw down a crucifix before the throne, asking whether the Monarchy was prepared, like Judas, to betray their Lord. And so Abravanel failed.

"What does it matter that those cruel monarchs later repented what they had done? It was too late, and it was the Ottoman Sultan who welcomed the Jews. He said, 'Thank you very much for the gold you sent me! You impoverished your country and enriched mine!'

"You didn't know nor did you see the pogroms of Kishinev, in tsarist Russia, the pogroms in Poland. You didn't see the Cossacks in Kiev! Our people, my children, will not find refuge until they have their own state where they will be independent.

"In all places we were persecuted—France, England, Germany, Prussia, Poland. There were many writers and men of the sciences. The Dreyfus affair! My children, what do they want the Jews to do? Not even assimilation brings us peace. Dreyfus was persecuted in liberal France...

"So, my children, I will not wait to make a homeland for us in this place. We cannot wait. I can only hope that someday that all men are our brothers, and all shall have equal rights. Our land should be paradise, and our motherland should be our humanity."

"You will forgive me, my father," I said, "but I believe we Jews only have one road, and that road is the union of all the people into one people. What does "Turkish" or "Greek" or "Jewish" mean? Does anyone think that the Jew has one eye in his head, like a Cyclops, and the Greek has two eyes? Does the earthworm find different grazing in the corpse of a Greek or a Jew? No! So, we should be brothers, there should not be differences among men. God, as you the rabbis say, gave us the world, the earth, and told us 'You can make it either paradise or hell.' We seem to prefer hell.

*****

Lizelda
A Sephardic Ballad
By Julia Ardetti

At the slope of a river
And the peak of a valley
I met my Lizelda,
Daughter of the emperor
Who came from the baths
From the cold-watered baths
To bathe herself and do her hair
To move to a light
Ladder that she made under
The windows, so that
She could go up and down as if it were
Her house.

She came across her father,
Are you okay, my daughter? Are you
Sick? Or are you pregnant?

I am neither sick nor pregnant.
I met Count Animale
Who fell in love with me.
Three nights he slept with her,
It seemed like three weeks.

If that is the case my daughter,
I will send for him to be killed.
Don't kill him, father.
Nor shall you wish to kill him.
The man is a boy and child
He wants to enjoy the world.
Banished from these lands

Nor eating the bread from here.

At the midnight hours,
Knights began to enter, their charge
Was strong, sparks began to fly.
Who is this enemy that
Wants to take the city?

I am not an enemy nor
Do I want to take the city. I want
My Lizelda, as a wife and as
An equal.

*****

"Mankind has determined we have a war every 20 years, and the last one? Oh, what a war! Oh my God! Yesterday at the movies I saw a film by Erich Maria Remarque, oh, what horrors are there in war! A father nurtures his son with a thousand worries, through sicknesses, through accident, through pain and danger, in order to create a useful human being. And then, in the end a machine gun kills many of those young men in the flower of their youth. That's war! And in the end, what do we see? Winnings and wounds come together. And all of that horror for the glory of a single man?

"Napoleon, that glorious man full of adventure. Didn't he get all of us and himself and the French people into war? What did he win? He went to Moscow and saw it burning, and so he turned back. What did he gain? Nothing. The people should pay attention, a lot of attention, in order to not put ignorant and contentedly selfish people at the head of a nation. Woe to the nation that holds such leaders in esteem, for it will end up being wiped from the face of the earth."

"No," said Aaron, my brother and the third son of Abraham, in a fanatical tone. Aaron was studying in a rabbinate that was part of the Jewish community in Salonika. He was an intelligent lad, only 15 years old, and when he turned of age, Abraham, our father had taught him the book of the Torah. "Our God that is in the heavens will not let us loose our people even of a race that is careless. It is the merit earned by Abraham, Isaac, and Jacob. Someday our God will redeem us, and He will gather us from the four corners of the earth, and He will send us to Israel." Aaron always stood by his speech before the neighborhood in which he promised, with an oath, to be a good Jew, a good citizen, and a good son to his father and mother.

Meanwhile, Djilda the second to the youngest, an eight year old, was quarreling with her little four year old brother Sabetico. Djilda whispered that girls were worth much more than boys. She also made it known to Sabetico that their uncle, who had a big belly never gave birth, whereas their mother Rachel, who hardly had a belly like that of their uncle, brought her and her brothers into the world. Sabetico, blushing with embarrassment, went to hide.

"My dear husband," Rachel, exclaimed to Abraham, "Don't you know that it's Passover and above all, on this first night, we should be happy? Why are you getting into such nonsense? These are matters and discussions that we are not the least interested in! Why should we care about the past? We look to the future for comfort. Water that has passed by doesn't turn a waterwheel. So, let's read the Seder message, and we'll eat, since these conversations can go on all night, discussing this and that. And what will we arrive at? Can we explain the evolution of the world? No."

"Mama, my dear Mama," I said, "you make some sense, but it is important that coming generations should live righteously. It is important that we shouldn't kill each other." Semaya hesitated, then added, "By the way, our world dates many millions of years back when the first men lived in caves, and slowly, slowly we have emancipated ourselves, and we become now what we are. We have airplanes, we have telephones, radios and wireless telegraphs, etc., etc. It's because of these advances that each generation has added a brick to the world's building. We must make the world in which we are travelers—this voyage that we make as men and not as beasts."

"Be quiet, Semaya!" yelled grandmother Oro. "You are against, heaven forbid, He who we will not name. You don't believe in anything. If you believed in God you wouldn't speak that way. God made the world, my grandson, in six days, and on the seventh day He rested. And it is from Abraham's time that the world can be dated. It doesn't date back millions of years. You are blaspheming."

"Dear Grandmother, I wasn't blaspheming, it's you that understood what I said backwards. I was only trying to say that the world was given to men by God, and that they should live without arguments and without war, that's what the prophet Isaiah said in chapter 3 or maybe 2, I don't recall..."

"And what did Isaiah say?"

"Isaiah says, well he more or less said this 3,000 years ago: And the people understood, and said, we will walk in the path of God, in the house of the God of Jacob, and let us walk in the straight path, and from Zion shall come the law, and it will speak of the God of Jerusalem, and He will judge among the people, and He will cause them to turn their weapons into ploughs, and their swords into spoons and knives to eat with, and city shall not lift a sword against city, and none will be taught to make war...

"You're old-fashioned, Grandmother, and times have changed. Our Bible has been translated into all languages, and what does it say? Many things, and so people take from this or that, and it makes religion very adaptable. When you see a preacher of Christ speak against other minorities, and above all else, against us, what should we think? Jesus said clearly, like Isaiah, that people should live by love not war. People who quote the Bible to argue otherwise are either playing the most dangerous game of our time or they don't understand what Christianity means.

"King Solomon was right when he said that without justice, there is evil. When we sin, those sins are punished by the heavens. Grandmother Oro, you know the mother of our Biblical Abraham said that we shouldn't trust in the goyim, they all want bad to befall us. So who is the darkness; who is the light?

"Well, dear Grandmother, I truly respect you because of your age. If I were speaking to someone else, I would fight with them, but you I respect because first, you are father's mother, and second, because of your age," Semaya concluded.

"We should not be afraid of these grey-haired ones, we are all brothers and sons of God," her other grandson Aaron said. Aaron was the yeshiva student, but he also continually attended meetings of political dissident groups. His opinions were a bit of everything, but according to him, even the groups with communist tendencies were all permissible and all had something to offer. While Aaron was only 15, he looked 18, and he already participated in subversive conversations with like minded people.

In contrast, I was calm by nature. We were literally at the opposite ends of the extreme—Aaron was small and thin, while I was tall and fat; Aaron was nervous and revolutionary, while I was calm and accommodating. I was studying in the community school, and our father Abraham said it was because he wanted me to become either a rabbi or a community teacher.

As for Aaron, Abraham saw that he was a brave young man flourishing in the milieu of Greeks and Jews where there were many ideas that Abraham felt weren't good for a Jew. Abraham had it in his head—and no one could get it out of his head—that the Jew is made of glass. If a stone hits glass, the glass will break. So, Abraham saw the future of Aaron as dark. At the synagogue he always begged God that He remove from that child the foolish ideas that he had because many times people from the neighborhood, and officers from the secret police came to condemn Aaron, and this filled his parents with fear and horror.

*****

All That God Created Was Created Perfectly
(A Sephardic Anecdote)

One day a resident of the village of Arnavutluk in Albania, was traveling from one village to another, in order to sell his merchandise. In a given moment he lies down to rest and notices that large watermelons grow on the ground while small Hanova olives grow on very large and tall trees.

Then the villager sat under the olive tree, and began to speak about it, saying, "I cannot understand why the religious ones say that God created everything perfectly, for is this not an imperfect thing? Large watermelons from 10 to 20 kilograms are growing from under the ground, and are supported by little roots, while little olives only grow to half a dram on such large trees."

As he argued with himself, a small wind began to blow, and suddenly an olive fell and hit him on the head. The olive hurt since it fell from a height of 20 feet.

"Oh boy," he exclaimed! "I have already sinned by speaking against God. God made everything with justice and perfection. What would happen if this olive had been a melon that weighed 20 kilos?

"God made everything in perfection!"

*****

Hillel and Shammai
(A Sephardic Lesson)

For many years the rival Talmudic schools of the House of Hillel and the House of Shammai debated a certain question, but they could not resolve it. The student of Shammai argues that it would have been far better for man had he never been created. The student of Hillel maintained that it was good that man had been created.

Finally, both schools concluded their controversy on a compromise: that it would have been far better for man had he never been created, but since he is already here, on earth, it is his obligation to make the best of it and live uprightly.

The Levy Family in 1927, (l. to r. back) Aaron, Semaya, (l. to r. front), Rachel, Djilda, Abraham.

Chapter 3: Camp Campbell

Kien de la miel manea algo se le apeya.
(He who moves from honey, will get stuck.)
- Sephardic Proverb

And so it came to be that after the Great Fire of 1917, the Jews of Salonika were dispersed near and far. Some chose to leave, to leave Salonika The Mother of Israel and move to other nearby enclaves: many became Djudios Turkos (Turkish Jews) by settling in Anatolia along the eastern coast of the Mediterranean, south of Istanbul. Others began to rebuild their old neighborhoods in Thessaloniki. However, the rebuilding was often delayed because the municipal authorities wanted to have a modern plan for the rebuilding rather than the rabbit burrows—the disorganized, disconnected, haphazard streets and lanes that existed previously, however charming the area might have been. As a result, a significant number of Salonika's Jews decided to remain in the camps where they had been sheltered immediately after the fire: in Dudular, in Kara-Isin and particularly in an area known as Camp Campbell.

Camp Campbell was a few kilometers outside of Salonika. The Salonika Jewish community, under the leadership of their honorable president, Yacovatchi Cazes, created an overwhelming pressure campaign in order to assure that there would at least be a dwelling place for those Jews who were arriving from the distant provinces of the Ottoman Empire that were falling to anti-Semitic Christians—Bosnia, Serbia, Bulgaria, and Crimea, as well as those families that were still without housing ever since the Great Fire in

1917. Finally, in 1928, a decision was made to purchase, from the English, the camp that was created from the barracks that housed the Allies during the First World War. But for many, this camp, so far from the city, was not a place where many of the Salonika Jews wanted to live.

So, the community and the council began to organize the neighborhood and the barracks in order to attract new residents. The Camp Campbell administrator, Mr. J. Romano, was able to impress the inhabitants that the area would be a good place to live, and within two months the settlement was filled with people coming to live there. But almost all the new inhabitants were porters and traveling salesmen, who barely managed to provide for their very large families, with the exception of a cafe owner—Haim Varsamo, my father Abraham only a carpenter but an advisor to the community, and the administrator, J.Romano. Almost all the rest suffered economically, and what a lamentable situation it was. In the days to come, many people living there went to bed hungry, and tuberculosis left its mark on the homes of these poor ones, many of whom were said to have the appearance of hungry dogs. Malaria also ravaged the area. There wasn't a single house that didn't have someone in the family suffering from tuberculosis or malaria or asthma.

The situation of these inhabitants was truly tragic because all of these families were Ben Porat-Yoseph (blessed sons of Joseph), meaning all the families were large. The doctor from Salonika, Dr. Pessah, didn't have enough help to handle the number of visits he had to make, and many times he couldn't even make all the visits needed and he was forced to leave patients untreated until the next day. Many times he requested help from Bikur Holim—the mutual aid society—for them to make another community doctor available, but they replied that their funds were already running low.

Such was the situation for these poor residents of Camp Campbell whose fate was determined to become so unfortunate. Their tragedy was compounded by the fact that many among them had very rich relatives, but those rich Jews had become proud of their class distinctions, and they very soon forgot about their poor relatives and they refused their poor cousins. The son of the rich brother would not know the son of the poor brother. Jewish solidarity was being weakened in Salonika, and not everything was done by traditional rules.

*****

A Cantor After Seventy.
(Sephardic Humor)

When God created the world, he first made animals and after that, man.

After he had created the dog, the dog asked God "What must I do in the world?" and God answered "You will have a master who will beat you if you will not obey him. You'll chew on bone and bark at the moon."

"How long will I live?"

"Seventy years" replied God.

"What!" cried the dog "Lead a dog's life for seventy years! Fifteen is enough!" And God agreed graciously.

Next, God created a horse. "What must I do in the world?" asked the horse.

God answered, "You will pull a load and get a good whipping for your trouble."

"How long will I live?"

"Seventy years."

"What?" cried the horse "Lead a horse's life for seventy years? Twenty five is enough!" and God agreed graciously.

Having created all the animals, God next made a Cantor. "What must I do in the world?" asked the Cantor", and God answered "You will have to sing at all the weddings and circumcision parties. When you chant the service in the synagogue, the members of the congregation will be in rapture. Your life will be an endless pleasure."

"How long will I live?" asked the Cantor.

"Seventy years," replied God

"Why that's too little!" cried the Cantor. "Almighty God! Grant me many more years!"

"You shall have more years," agreed God graciously.

But where could God find for him the years beyond three-score and ten? He could only give it to him from the years allotted to the dog and the horse.

Therefore, good friend, if you listen to a Cantor who is above seventy, don't be surprised if he howls like a dog, and if you eat with him don't be surprised if he gorges like a horse!

*****

The Jewish community of Salonika was not only divided by class and political differences (some believed in assimilation, some were Zionists, some were communists and other leftists), the creation of Camp Campbell also occurred simultaneously with the rise of a fascist, nationalist organization, the 3 epsilons—the National Union of Greece—that had grown in power when, in 1912, Salonika had been annexed by the new Greek nation state. The National Union was accused of having a serious anti-Semitic ideology although it was said, somewhat disingenuously, that since Greece was a democracy, there couldn't be fascism or anti-Semitism. But the signs were clear to those who chose to see them.

For all of those reasons, there arose, within the Salonika Jewish community a large opposition group that was strongly opposed to sending Jews to new settlements so far outside the city. With great wisdom and foresight they predicted, all too accurately, what the consequences of building and maintaining Camp Campbell would entail—both an enormous expense, and the dilution of political power within the increasingly Greek city of Thessaloniki. But, the argument that shelter was needed for so many displaced Jews prevailed, and compassion carried the day.

*****

The Dove
A Sephardic Poem

Open your window.
You will see a dove.
Treat it with love,
For it is a person.

I wake up in the morning.
I sit in the garden,
Like that mother
Who lost her son.
The son is gone.
The father searches for him.

For the most part,
The tiny dove stays with the mother.
You are so small, give me your
love when I am alive...

The stars in the sky.
One and one and one and two.
They do not have the finesse,
like the two of us have.

God created all that is brown.
The silversmith made all that is white.
Let the people of the earth live,
for them I die.

I love you and I adore you.
I kept you in my dream.
I want to marry you.
I didn't confront God.

You are so small, full of love.
Give me your love, when I am alive.

*****

Ah, but if only we could have truly seen the cost of our love and compassion! Camp Campbell initially sheltered around 116 families. That came to about 500 people, because all of the poor families had so many children. They wanted a school, a teacher, a rabbi, a ritual slaughterer, a mohel to perform circumcisions, all of those elements that made for a true Jewish community. Furthermore, they also needed a paid community administrator. And then there was the question of water. In order to make sure that there was water, they needed a full-time employee who worked from 6:00 am to 4:00 pm making sure the pumps were turned off and on, and that they were in good condition.

From such small details are great debates created, and there were always great debates in the Jewish councils of Salonika. However none of these debates ever appeared in the newspapers like the English-language Action and Truth or the French-language L'Independent and Le Progrès so that the goyim would not be aware of the battles taking place within the community. But the Judeo-Spanish press was filled with invective. It was like the Battle of Plevna [a great battle of the Russo-Turkish War] was being fought over and over again, and there were days when it seemed that the entire community was consumed in the conflict. The police were called more than once to quell mob scenes.

As a result, the residents of Camp Campbell became a wound on the larger community. Residents often didn't go to work because of the distance, and it became the responsibility of the larger community to give them alms; there were other, even more brash ones, who simply took money from the communal chest. You could count on your fingers the very few who worked and who therefore did not need to be helped by the larger community.

Then there came a time when the Salonika president, Mr. Liaom Benoziglio, declared that it was necessary that every family have a little house. At the beginning of Pesach, matzo was given to everyone freely, and countless sums of money were given to each individual family. Everyone benefited from these policies, even those who didn't need the help.

For the community, then, there were two solutions that could bring an end to the agony: either close down the new settlement, or let Camp Campbell evolve, and develop as it might.

It was allowed to develop.

*****

The Piece of Cheese
(A Sephardic Lesson)

One day two cats robbed a piece of cheese from a marketplace and were killing each other over it! One of them said, "Meow, I risked myself to take it and you didn't do anything!"

The other one said, "Meow, what risk was there to snatch it?"

Afterwards they continued to fight and blood soon came about. "Meow!"

"Why are we killing each other? Let's go to the judge and ask that he help us to reason."

They crawled and crawled and finally arrived at the judge, who was also a feline who asked, "Why did you come? Can't you agree with one another?"

After they explained everything, the judge arrogantly said that she would bring them a scale. "Do you see how we did well in coming to the judge to judge us?" one cat says to the other. "So that she may give us equal pieces, she wants us to bring her a scale."

After much agony, the cats bring the scale. So the judge takes a knife and cuts the cheese into 2 pieces. She takes one part and puts it into one of the scale's plates and does the same for the other. Of course, she didn't cut the two pieces equally, for each time one was heavier. So, the judge cut one more and put it in her other hand. And she kept doing this until the pieces of cheese went right into her throat without giving the two cats anything but the scale that they had brought her.

"Meow! Meow!"

Djilda Levy (right) and friend before the Campbell Pogrom, 1930

Chapter 4: The Campbell Pogrom

Esperando el pogrom en la escuridad haze mas mucho espantar del actual pogrom.
(There is no greater fear than waiting nervously in the dark for a pogrom attack.)
- Sephardic Proverb

At the beginning of April, 1930, the baker for the neighborhood of Camp Campbell, a generous Greek named Anhoni who refused to become part of a pogrom because he was a friend to the Jews—he ate with us and lived with us—gathered all the Jews of the neighborhood together in Haim Varsamo's café at the entry to the neighborhood. He wanted to put us on alert that there was a serious danger arising that threatened the residents of the settlement. According to what he had heard, Camp Campbell was going to be burned by the Ethniki Enosis Ellados, the National Union of Greece, the anti-Semitic organization, with its intrigues and machinations against the Jews of Salonika. The EEE's weapon of choice was turning out to be barrels of petroleum.

"Comrades!" said my brother, Aaron, who had allied himself with the communists and other left-wing groups, "The danger is real—they are threatening to burn us alive, like rats. We need to organize ourselves; we need to collaborate with the Greek anti-fascist factions because they are the only ones who will truly help us in the fight against these terrorists!

"There will be new massacres like those of Kishinev and the Ukraine. We must be ready; we must have confidence in our strength! This danger of being burned alive should be met with our cold blood!"

"No my brothers," exclaimed Abraham, who was the teacher and the rabbi of the neighborhood and represented the moderate faction, "it is useless to meet violence with violence. Tomorrow we will send a delegation of residents to the president of the community requesting that he go to Governor General Gonatas in order to have the Governor save us from this threat. If we have patience and trust in the Greek community and its leaders, then no evil will befall us, with God's help…" It was always the rabbi who threw water on the smoldering fire.

"Enough, already! We didn't say that we would only count on our own strength," exclaimed many voices in the crowd. The matter, then, was put to a vote and it was decided unanimously that the next day a delegation would go to the home of the president of the community, Mr. Benoziglio, and the delegates would make Benoziglio understand the danger and the consequential need to act. The delegation was made up of the Shamash, my father Avram Levy, the administrator Joseph Romano, David Lea, Haim Barsiano, and Peppo Zimbal who was the mechanic for the water system in the neighborhood. They were told to bring concrete reports back to the residents the same day.

My father addressed the president: "Mr. President, we, a delegation of residents from Camp Campbell have come to tell you that there are serious rumors flying through our community that there is immediate danger that the pogromists from Ethniki Enosis Ellados will burn us like rats in the camp. Fellow Jews came yesterday from the city and confirmed it to us. True Greek friends have also warned us. They have counseled us to take the necessary measures so that we can save our lives. Yesterday, barrels of gasoline were sent to the business address of the neighborhood baker, Anhoni. He told us about the gasoline, and he refused to be an accomplice to this filthy organization."

"Don't be afraid, my children, we are here. We won't let this happen," said the naïve community president in all sincerity.

"You don't understand. You come here and live in Camp Campbell! We're already here!" shouted David Lea, who represented the left-wing groups.

"I am going to Governor General Gonatas. I will tell him all of this, and return tomorrow when I will give you his answer," said Mr. Benoziglio.

*****

He Who Does Well In Life Deserves To Be Praised.
(A Sephardic Lesson)

The wife says to her husband, "Look, we must take care of your old man until he gives us all of his life's earnings."

The son thought about this, and soon after agreed with his wife. The father finally accepted he should give his fortune to his son while he was still alive. This they agreed upon among one another, for "my son will do no wrong."

The next day when the father gave all his fortune to his son, poverty soon began for the father.

He was allowed to eat only half of what he used to, his house was rented out, and they left the father one little space in the kitchen. The father was dying of grief. Not only this, but his daughter-in-law beat him.

One day, he called his son and complained to him, but his words went in one ear and out the other. So, one day the father decided to teach his son a lesson.

He went to a money exchanger, bought a bag of fake liras and every night when his daughter-in-law arrived, he began to toss the bags of fake liras around on the table, counting them and arranging them in piles. The daughter-in-law, hearing the sound of money, said to her husband, "Did you know that your old man still has liras?"

So, the son recommended that they change their behavior with the father, and they returned things to the way they were in the beginning. The father began to eat well again and get out more often. He was able to wash himself daily, and the daughter-in-law even gave him a kiss each day.

"Oh Lord, the things that money can do," exclaimed the father, adding, "the French say it well, 'money makes war'."

So, the old man lived a very nice life with his son, and everyone in the congregation took the son for an exemplary man. It is only when the old man died that they found his liras, his fake liras.

*****

At 11:00 in the morning a carriage took the community president to the Governor General.

Benoziglio said to Governor Gonatas: "Excellency, I need to bring you up to date with what is happening at Camp Campbell. Ethniki Enosis Ellados wants to burn down Camp Campbell, and since that area is far from the city proper, we beg that the property and that the lives of my brethren be protected by the state."

"Not a hair of any Jew will be touched. Be calm, and tell the residents to be calm as well. I will give the order to the police to go on horseback and to maintain order there," said Gonatas. "This is the work of malcontents. Be calm and don't worry about anything. But, if something should occur, come to my home at any hour, and we will go there together." It was with those comforting words ringing in his ears that Mr. Benoziglio left the governor's office and returned to speak to the delegation from Camp Campbell.

"My children!" said the arrogant Benoziglio, "As I promised you, I went and spoke at length with the governor, who said for us to be calm, and not a hair of any Jew will be touched, so calm yourselves. He also said that a troop of officers will arrive on horseback to guard you. Don't worry about things!"

When the news of Benoziglio's meeting with Gonatas was brought back to the community, my mother Rachel didn't trust the information. She was scared and so she said to my father, "Avram, my dear lifelong companion, get moving! Go to your cousin's house, go to lawyer Abraham Levy's and tell him what awaits us. See if he can put us up as his guests for one or two weeks, until this storm passes."

She sensed that my father was reluctant to do anything. "You know that we have children, don't you? Aaron came home today scared and out of breath? He told me that everything Gonatas told Benoziglio is a lie. He says that everyone is plotting against us!"

But my father said: "And what will my cousin do for me? Don't you know him? Even if he wants to take us in, his wife won't want to. And then we'll be obliged to never speak to them again. Knowing this, my dear Rachel, you go and speak to his wife, and I will be in charge of at least preparing our luggage so that we can be ready."

Students from the Jewish Ecole Francais before the Campbell Pogrom. 1929.

Rachel, Avram's lifelong companion, was accomplished at convincing people to listen to her and getting them to respond to her. That was why my father begged her to go to his cousin's and he hoped that God would be with her.

When my mother arrived at Abraham Levy's house in the city, she said: "Abraham Levy! We hardly ever see you and we have never asked you for anything, but in these moments of anguish we ask that you protect us. You already know that we are in grave, life-threatening danger. This is about the life or death of your cousin's family."

"And what do you ask of me, my dear Jewess?" replied the lawyer Levy.

"You are a powerful man and you have a house here in the city. The pogromists won't ever attack you. I ask of you, I beg of you that you let us stay in your home for one or two weeks!"

"Look, my good lady, what you're asking me isn't possible for me to do. I have, as you know, many cousins and many nephews. I can't house them all here. If I let you come, I'll have to let the others come as well."

"Then you must welcome all the others into your home as well. You are our first cousin, a close relative. In these times you must show your friendship. You know what the family did and what we gave so that you could become a lawyer! And with all that, you still say no! Listen, I don't want to throw all of this in your face, but out of necessity, in this grave time, I am obliged to."

The lawyer Levy was taken aback. "Well! But...but...okay, I'll...ask the opinion...of my wife..." He went to his wife's side and whispered a few words in her ear.

"Never in my life!" his wife was adamant. " I won't allow them to enter my house. A thousand times no, never in my life!"

"That's enough out of you," my mother said to her. "Remember that if you find yourself still married it's thanks to us! When your husband wanted to leave you, we talked to him so that he wouldn't. And now you are doing this to me! Despicable! For now, it is in our garden rain will fall, but you can't know what tomorrow will bring."

"Come on, you snake!" replied the wife. "That's enough out of you! You have brought a cemetery to our door! You were always this way! There's no way to get what you want from us, so go back from where you came from. You heard me! Go!"

If a bullet had struck my mother at that moment it would have been nothing to her; she could only think of how many things the Levy family had done for him, and with what means they had helped him. And then, in the hour when the rest of the family was in need, the lawyer and his wife were turning their backs on the rest of the family.

Rachel left, bitter-hearted, and in such distress, that instead of taking the tram to return to Campbell, she took the tram to the bazaar, and it wasn't until she arrived at Veneselos Street that she realized the mistake that she had made.

*****

When the Rich Promise
(A Sephardic Lesson)

A rich tobacco merchant from the city of Salonika took his carriage and went with his servant Ahmed to Albania to the well stocked tobacco marketplace located in the inner area of Macedonia. There was so much snow and continuous cold there that the horses couldn't trot along, so the merchant and his servant Ahmed were obliged to remain in their comfortable, yet cold, carriage.

At midnight, the merchant said, "Ahmed, if God keeps us alive tonight, let's then go to and order 10,000 cords of wood for the poor people of our community back in Salonika, since it is winter and the temperature must be frigid.

"Okay," said Ahmed.

After some time the rich man and the servant returned to Salonika. When they entered their warm, heated house, the merchant remembered his promise and said to his servant, "Ahmed! Don't order the wood! The temperature has risen here in Salonika. We don't need the poor people to use all that wood when the temperature is this hot."

"Very well, Sir," said Ahmed, while smiling in disbelief at the rich merchant's easily dismissed vows to help the poor.

*****

Now, there is no greater fear than the fear that comes from waiting, nervously, for an attack. Those who were the most frightened from the neighborhood fled from the moment that Andrea the grocer, and Anhoni the baker told us their news. But those that left either had money or relatives in the city who would take them in. As to the rest of us?

Unfortunately most of us stayed and waited for the attack. However, some felt it was their obligation to flee with as much as they could carry, and stay with whomever they could. These people were always the distrustful ones in the neighborhood. They didn't have faith in anyone, and it was because of this distrust that they wanted to flee during this terrible time. But it was possible that nothing would happen, and that all of the panic was due to nothing more than alarming rumors. Maybe it was true, as it was said, that the democratic Greeks wouldn't beat a Jew. But what if there were violence?

The administrator, Mr. J. Romano stayed only to show the people he was courageous. Our father Abraham and our family had nowhere to go after what our cousin said to Rachel.

"Where would we go, my dear Rachel? The Governor General, isn't stirring from his place. We will be here, and what God has determined, we cannot flee," said Abraham.

"At least the children, our beloved children. Let them go to the city shelter, or, for a few nights, to a hotel."

"We won't leave you alone," my brother Aaron and I exclaimed. "Your fortune will be our fortune."

"I will defend all of us," exclaimed Aaron in a loud voice. "I have Greek friends that will come to help us. Don't you worry about a thing. Here, take this revolver that Costa the chauffeur gave me. There are five rounds, and I have more here in my bag."

"Aaron my beloved," said our mother, "he gave you a revolver! You are just a chick, newly hatched out of the shell! You became a part of the minyan only two years ago! Put the revolver into the cabinet! You know that our community says that whoever has firearms will be imprisoned, and above all, it is especially dangerous for you who are under constant suspicion."

"Mama! I beg you not to offend me with your love and concern. We find ourselves in a state of defense and we must do whatever is needed, even use weapons if necessary."

"Yes, my dear son! You're right in what you are saying! But, do we need this weapon now that the police, both on foot and by horse, are going to protect us? Leave it. We don't want to respond to violence with violence. You know that we are few and they are many. Our religion always provides us with its strength. Don't they know that we are Jewish!"

"It kills me to tell you, my dear mother, that you are very naïve! And if I am a Jew, so what? Should the human race draw distinctions among its members? Is it that I, as a Jew, have one eye in my head and they have two? Does the hungry lion in the jungle draw a distinction between the Greek and the Jew? No, mother, these ideas you have will only do us harm. We should trust in our strength, and not wait for the community president to again go to the governor. Yes, yes, I know the governor already gave his word, etc. etc. But, take a look now, tonight, what are the president and the governor general doing? They are at some tea party in honor of someone or another, and it hardly matters to either of them what awaits us!

"You accuse me of subversive ideas because of the truths that I'm telling you. And well… you are mistaken. I want justice and the rest of this arguing doesn't matter much to me. I'm neither a communist, which you accuse me of being, nor do I have subversive ideas. I'm just rebelling. Against what? Why? It's wrong that in the 20th century, these injustices exist! These abominable crimes, this atrocity of men against their brethren.

"Mother, into this bizarre world we all arrived with the same rights. We have our equal place under the sun; we are all travelers. Just as the shadow that passes, like the wind that blows, once we are travelers for whatever reason, can this journey we make on the earth have no value?"

"Come on! Be quiet, Aaron!" said our mother. "Always talking, talking! These are theories that are only written on paper—in real life they are wrong. Why don't you ask us? If you're going to ask the wrong people, you're going to change from the way you were raised. You will go crazy."

"Aaron," said our father, "only when we Jews have our own homeland, with the help of God, will the Jew then be at rest. For now, we are in captivity. We are at the forefront of anti-Semitism. From the beginning of our exile, the world was made in this way. And only when God reigns over us will we rest.

"As you know we gave light to the world. It was from us that the Christians copied the Bible. And don't you forget that we gave them Jesus too, for the first thing Jesus says is, 'I came to reinforce and fulfill the 10 commandments of Rabbi Moses.' Although I too must ask, where is the 'love thy neighbor as thyself?' Where is the 'what you don't want for yourself you don't want for the person in front of you?'

"Now my children, there are those that want to burn us. They don't even believe in the strictest things their religion says to believe in. So, children, have patience and faith in God. He is the only one who will save us and he will save us from all. Isn't every nation that challenged or continues to challenge the chosen people condemned to disappear from the earth? How many nations challenged the Jews and weren't punished?

"Where are the Philistines? Where is Haman? Where is Amalek? Torquemada! The Roman Empire? So, my children, always have hope in God, and the Holy One, blessed be He, will save us from the evil ones.

"Here, in Greece, the prime minister, Eleftherios Venizelos has anti-Semitic politics. But, it is this nation that will one day be brought down. Why do I say that it will be brought down? Because Greece left the straight and forward path. It left the religious teachings that Christians preach and think they believe.

"So, my children, to work, and God be with us! You, Semaya, will take care of Djilda your little sister, Sabetico and your mother. You, Aaron, will watch so that they don't burn our home, and I will read psalms from the prayer book so that God will protect us from all evil. Pay attention also to the synagogue! They mustn't burn the books. Take care also of your grandmother Oro; don't let anything happen to her. And, children, be very aware of our neighbor's house, since her older son is serving in the military and her husband is in the hospital. Watch and make sure everything is done the right way!"

*****

Hope
(A Sephardic Poem)

> Good weeks we see coming,
> We leave to welcome them,
> So that God lets us live,
> Us and all of Israel.

The great Lord with his grace
Sends us much fortune.
He doesn't send us evil nor worry,
To us and all of Israel.

Come all fortunate ones
Your name we will bless
And from you we will ask
For the salvation of Israel.

You who are our heavenly father.
You send the shepherd to us
For it will be our sign
To us and all of Israel.

Lord, give us your blessing
With good conditions
Show us salvation.
We are ready
For what we have been through
Send us to the anointed
Messiah of Israel.

*****

It was nighttime, a night in the springtime. The trees were beginning to blossom, to put forth their first flowers on that May morning in 1930. The stars were out and the half moon, shone its silvery beams on the earth below. On this night full of traps and betrayals, the murmuring in the streets put fear into people's hearts. The mewling caused by the hungry stray cats made one tremble. The tragedy of waiting for the attack was very scary for everyone. All our voices begged for the pogrom begin so we would not have to wait any longer. The hungry dogs barked because they knew that something serious was coming. What a difference, oh

God, between nature's brilliance and fruitfulness in the spring, and the agony of the pogrom!

At our house, everything was ready; we had left behind the idea of getting help, and we were preparing our defense. Everyone in the family had a mission that could end their lives. Even little Djilda had a mission to undertake. She asked her mother, "Why will they hurt us? Why do they want to burn us? Wasn't I good? Is it because I'm not going to school? But yesterday I received a gold star from the teacher! And I..., I eat everything you give me, so why do they want to burn us?"

Djilda's questions and her words that were accompanied by waving hands and scissoring feet affected our mother Rachel's emotions and caused tears to spring to her eyes. But she forced herself to hide her low spirits from the child and above all to hide her fear.

"Stop, my dear, nothing will happen. The God of Israel will save us. Now make sure that you remember to say the Shemah."

In this manner Djilda became happier, and above all had a clear conscience, knowing she was good and ate her food and had received a gold star, and for that reason nothing would happen.

*****

Petropolemo (The War of the Stones)
(A Sephardic Story
by Itzhak Ben-Rubi)

In 1910, the Jews of the small community of Seres, a city in Macedonia, 90 kilometers from Salonika, were getting ready for the upcoming holidays of Rosh Hashana and Yom Kippur, and also for the opening of the schools. Books and bags, and new shoes for the children had to be bought. The parent's frustration was transmitted to their children, already sad since their vacation was coming to an end.

When little David, well-dressed, brushed, hugged, kissed, sick of well-wishes from his parents, grandparents, uncles and aunts, went on his way to school, he felt like a soldier leaving for the front-lines. David had just turned 10 years old and already he knew the disturbances of mankind.

Not very happy, he continued on his way toward the school. School didn't scare him, it was the sense of anxiety and solemnity in the air that pierced his heart—the sounds that the neighborhood cantor played in the mornings from a strange instrument, the shofar, getting ready for the Days of Repentance, the first rains of the fall season. All of these things brought about tears in the eyes

Classmates and teachers from Jewish school of Altcheh before the Campbell Pogrom, 1929.

of David, a sensitive soul. And with these feelings, Dave passed the entrance of the school.

Many writers and poets have painted with many bright colors the happiness that comes with the start of classes. Little Dave did not know about this happiness. He lived his own life.

In his seat, in class, he felt a wave of sadness fill the room. This wave seemed to come from the movements of the black beard of the schoolteacher, Yitzak Avinu. His beard seemed to cover, as if from a black cloud, the gracious little heads of the children.

And the song, repeated by the students, played melancholically in Dave's heart:

"Speak with your mother,
for her son died,
The son you gave birth to
when you were 90 years old"
It was because of the fire
and the knife."

Little David couldn't understand, for in his innocent soul, this song that he and his young classmates had to repeat, was tied to an event over 4000 years old from the history of his people. He felt in his own flesh the knife and the fire and he wanted to run into the street to stop this crime so that the boy wouldn't die and the mother wouldn't have this pain, at the age of 90!

Fortunately, the marbles of the multiple colors that fell out from the pocket of his friend Victor, the laughter of the other students, and the shouts of the teacher, distracted him from such sad thoughts.

Then bell announcing that recreation time was finally approaching made David, at his tender age, smile. In the large garden of the school, he played "pass and throw," "three jumps," and "pits," and above all, he played with the marbles of rainbow colors which fascinated him. They also played "cops and robbers."

The bad children played "throw stones" despite the principal of the school's objection to this and the severe punishments given for playing this game, considered a crime. But the throwers of the stones had in their heart an inferiority complex because these Jewish kids resented the pain they felt at not being able to respond to the invitation of the Greeks to join them in this "war of stones."

In the customs and traditions of the Greek population in those times, petropolemo, the battle of the stones, was like soccer or tennis. Very rarely did a parent complain when their child was hurt while playing in the battle of stones. About other things there were scandals, but when it came to the battle of the stones, they remained silent, accepting the laws of the game, confined by tradition like the great men of yesterday and today accepted and accept the laws that govern war in the world.

It is in this way that Jewish children, despite their smallness in numbers, accepted the situation as a matter of fact, for their parents didn't understand the need and the honor that there was in order to respond to this battle—a provoking declaration of war with fighting on two fronts: the stones of the Greeks and the beatings from the parents. The Jewish children lost all of the battles, and they lost them many times before even starting because they were forced to go and hide from fear of their parents.

What wind of courage, escaped from the waves of time, came to whisper in the ears of these children—that they were descendants from the ancient towns of war? Who would believe upon hearing that their ancestors Moshe, Saul, David, Samson and Bar-Kohba wielded powerful weapons? A mystery!

The president of the Jewish community issued a strict order that students of all the classes had to meet up on Monday at 5 o'clock in the evening, in the little field of the Jewish quarter to push back the Greeks with a counter attack in the battle of stones in case that, according to their practices, the Greeks would start an offensive against the Jewish quarter.

And so the community of Seres prepared their children for the reality of the pogroms to come, and Little David was destined to learn an even more disturbing lesson about the behavior of mankind.

*****

In the Campbell neighborhood the group in charge of our defense included two brave Greeks. They drew up the plans, and truly the neighborhood had taken on the appearance of a war zone. The signal of alarm was biscocho (biscuit) and as soon as the alarm was given, everyone was to be ready; that is, those of who remained, the poorest ones, who didn't have any place to go in the city, and who were obliged to confront the pogrom. You had to see these heroes who spoke with such courage, those that made the plans and encouraged the crowd.

Greece must raise up a memorial bigger than the one that they put up for the great patriots and liberators of a war! Those two were Greeks who were heroes and good Christians. They didn't leave off even a punctuation mark of the law of Jesus—'don't kill, love thy neighbor as thyself, and what you don't wish for yourself don't wish for the person in front of you.'

The shock of confronting our enemy in a face-to-face fight is less than that of nervously awaiting them. The attack was expected that night in May of 1930, and that night is engraved upon the memories of those who lived through it, engraved forever in our memories. How different, or rather how contrary it is to speak of nature, oh God, nature—a clear sky full of stars, not a single cloud covered the half-moon—this, in comparison with the state of alarm in the neighborhood, the horror. On the one hand there was blessed nature, which was promised to the poor man who awaited justice and the right to live under the sun, which God gave to the son of man. On the other hand, there was the terror that men brought against each other.

My father said: "I see that you are trembling, my dear Rachel. Why? You should set the example for the children so they won't be afraid. What is the point of fear? Can you stop anything with crying? No," exclaimed Abraham, "a thousand times no. During the fire of 1917, you were more courageous. Don't you remember fleeing from the flames when you were in your final month of pregnancy, that you fell on the train tracks and the locomotive would have crushed you if by luck you hadn't had a spiritual presence with you that moved you off of the tracks? Why don't you show the same courage now?"

"My dear husband, I myself don't worry about dying, but the children! Oh God! When I think of them and about all that awaits us, I get worked up. I don't even know what I want to do…"

Suddenly Aaron entered our house, out of breathe from running, but struggling to speak. Finally he said, "Father! They're coming here! About 500 meters from our house there is a band of ignorant people from the Ethniki Enosis Ellados. I must warn the baker so that he can warn the others so that they can defend us."

"Don't be frightened and don't be startled," counseled my father. "You know that when the delegation went to the community council president, Mr. Benoziglio, he assured us that he had the promise of the Governor General himself that he would send the police here to defend us, and that not a hair of anyone's head would be touched. Let us have faith, my children, in our leaders."

"And what a miserable leader," spat Aaron. "Here we have them at the door. Are we still with hope? All that's left is to defend ourselves."

But then, the police on horseback did arrive. They took up combat positions and announced that no inhabitants should leave their houses. That leaving was absolutely prohibited, and those who did would risk their lives.

My father was triumphant. "You see, my children, how Governor General Gonatas kept his word? There! They will defend us, and the pogromists will see the police and will go back to where they live."

*****

When There Is A Pogrom
(A Sephardic lesson)

An officer of Tsar Nicholas of Russia presents himself to the Great Rabbi and says, "Rabbi, I represent our dear Tsar Nicholas. For tomorrow, we ask that you give a sermon in the synagogue, praising our tsar and asking for God to grant him a long life.

"But...!" the rabbi responded.

"But nothing!" the officer said. "It is an order!"

The rabbi decided to speak with the rabbinate.

After many a debate, 90% did not want the rabbi to give this speech considering that the community had just suffered through another pogrom. Yet, if the rabbi did not give the speech, his refusal would have more negative consequences for the life of the Jewish community. So the rabbi said, "I will speak only in Hebrew, and only the teacher of our congregation knows Hebrew."

After speaking half an hour entirely in Hebrew, the officer of the Tsar's army who heard the speech and who didn't understand anything, wanted an explanation and went to the teacher for it.

"Tell me, teacher, why does the rabbi say yimach shemo every time he mentions the name of Tsar Nicholas? What does this mean?"

"Ah, my dear officer. I will tell you that in Hebrew, which is God's language, and for which only He can understand, it means long life." Which of course was untrue since yimach shemo means, 'may his name be obliterated'.

But the officer, fully pleased, went to convey the news to the Tsar.

*****

Soon the first flames began to burn, and the citizens were extremely worried. They saw for themselves the terrible results of the fascist newspaper Makedonia and its collaborating writer, Fardis, mouthpieces that riled up the people's feelings each day with anti-Semitic diatribes.

First, the wooden barracks were burned, one after another. The police, tried in vain to push back the pogromists, but they made no headway against the snarling, seething crowd. For one thing, they were unsure about what to do. The police that kept watch at the north end of the quarter threatened death to the inhabitants who left their homes that were erupting in flames. What did they care if the families were burned like rats when the police themselves felt threatened by the crowd?

Anhoni, the baker, like the lion he was, threw himself into the fight. With his hands, with his mouth, and with all his might he tried to pacify the furious crowd of poor proletarians who were burning out their co-proletarians who were as poor as they were. And not only that, the fanatic crowd included a religious authority with a cross in his hand. Oh, God, where was Yeshua of Bethlehem? Where were his fine words—love your neighbor like your self. What hypocrisy, or better yet what tragi-comedy were his representatives enacting?

A bullet to Anhoni's head, was the attackers' response. Anhoni, the good man, fell with the first bullet of the assassins. Then a pogromist killed the first Jew to flee from the flames, a certain Leon Juda, who left his house to save the baker who called for help.

The flames now spread throughout the quarter, starting from the north gate where the crowd first entered and attacked the house of the administrator, Mr. J. Romano. Everything was destroyed with clubs and axes; Romano fainted from a beating, and the women of his household were humiliated by the attackers, one at a time. "Here! Jewess, that's good enough for you!" they shouted as they spit on the women.

It was a terrifying scene. Many of the inhabitants did leave their homes and managed to save themselves from the flames, but the crowd attacked and mistreated them. This threatening scene truly resembled the pogroms of Kishinev. It was a disgrace to the 20th century, and above all a stain upon the brilliant history of the Greek people who are and always were liberal and tolerant, that they allowed this filthy organization Ethniki Enosis Ellados under the cloak of nationalism to commit this vandalism.

When the pogrom was at its zenith, three quarters of the area was already burned, and nothing could be heard except the lamentations of the attacked families. And so I ask, did the sinister Gonatas succeed in maintaining order? Was it true that not a single hair of any Jew was harmed when that night of betrayal came?

Frankly, the foreign newspapers did exaggerate what happened, but there's no fire without flames. The American journals were the worst, reporting that close to 100 synagogues were burned and that many people were killed. That was not true. But the truth was bad enough because nothing at all should have occurred. One synagogue was burned along with all its books and scrolls. The settlement's small school was burned. Dozens of inhabitants were seriously hurt. A number of married women and young virginal girls were raped. Many houses were burned including the houses of the rabbi and the administrator. Romano and his family were rushed to the hospital, as was the rabbi and his wife, both of whom who were abused. The administrator's wife was raped and abused. Semaya, Aaron, Djilda, and Sabetico, had hidden themselves in a cellar and that way avoided the abuse of the pogromists, but the house at the front belonging to David Nathan the barber was completely burned, and his wife and children were seriously hurt. Joseph, his son who is the head of the family, wasn't touched because that night he stayed at his mother-in-law's house, and that house wasn't attacked. The baker was killed, also the cousin of Rabbi Abraham, Leon Juda was killed at the very moment that he left his house to save the baker. But it must also be said that all of the journals of Salonika, with one anti-Semitic exception that remained silent, condemned the pogromists.

*****

The Traveller
(A Sephardic Ballad)

He took arm in arm
Just as he went to sleep
Let the morning dawn
I will prepare a good outfit for you
And I will make you a scarf.
That fits well with your outfit.

I want to go, mother
Through these fields I will go
The grass of these fields I will eat as my bread
And the tears of my eyes I will drink as my water.
And in the middle of those fields
I will build a palace.

Every passing man
That arrives will know it.
I will tell him of my hardships
And he will also tell me.
If his are fewer
I will learn patience from him
If mine are greater
I will hand myself a knife.

Chapter 5: After The Pogrom
Para un mal hombre, hay un mas mal hombre.
(For every bad man he finds an even worse man.)
- Sephardic Proverb

And so, on the day after the horrors of the Campbell Pogrom, Mr. Liaom Benoziglio, president of the community council, called an emergency meeting of the council's members in order to make decisions—first, about the fate of the inhabitants of Campbell now sequestered in their homes or in other settlements, and second, the fate of all the other community settlements that sheltered three-quarters of the poor and middle-class population, as well as all of the 60,000 brethren that lived in Salonika.

The Jewish deputies to the Greek legislature were also requested to attend the emergency meeting because the alarming chaos created by the Campbell pogrom was felt deeply by all the Jewish people in the city, rich and poor without exception. During that night in Campbell, Ethniki Enosis Ellados had even put Jewish stars on the doors of all of the Jewish homes. Anxiety was rampant throughout the city.

Benoziglio, Benico Saltiel, Avram Levy, Isaac Angel, David Chunina, Peppo Chenio, Leon Gattegno, Isaac Altabesh, Haimaki Koen, and the Jewish deputies to the Greek legislature, David Matalom, Asher Malla, and Alberto Chenio attended the meeting.

Immediately, Benoziglio, began to speak: "Gentlemen, members of the council, it is with a feeling of great sadness, and everyone of you experiences that same sadness, that I speak to you today. This sadness, this grieving that has fallen upon us is also shared by His Excellency, Governor General Gonatas. I have spoken with him, and I told him of all that happened yesterday. He promised me that all would be well, and that he has charged the police with taking appropriate measures.

The Chief of Police, Mr. Calo Christianolis, also promised me the same thing, and it is also with great sadness that he has received the news about what happened. He added that he didn't want to take any initiative on his own, or any steps regarding the situation, or measures to silence the anti-Semitic press without first having the agreement and cooperation of all concerned. He asked for our cooperation in order to make a decision and then to work together to implement that decision.

"Mr. President," exclaimed Alberto Chenio, "given what you told us yesterday, that our concerns about a possible pogrom were the cause of all the commotion, and that the settlement inhabitants were exaggerating things so we remained calm in our homes, what else did you expect to happen because of your efforts?

"No! Dear member and friend, I did my duty. As soon as I heard this fuss and as soon as I saw with my own eyes the Jewish symbols that were marked on the doors of the Jewish homes, and as soon as I read the vicious article from the Makedonia newspaper, I imagined that something terrible was going to happen in that far-off community settlement. That is exactly why, together with the chancellor, Mr. Daout Levy, we went to the Governor General and told him everything, yes everything in all its detail, because you felt that Gonatas wasn't giving any importance to the danger. And in order to be more certain that the settlement was protected, I had him telephone the Chief of Police, Mr. Calo Christianolis, and I heard with my own ears what was said between them. Gonatas told me with a smile, that 'not a single hair of any Jew's head will be touched.' And that was the way that we, that is to say, the delegation, left—pleased with the Governor General's promises. Pleased, I could say, but I had a presentiment that something was going to happen, and it happened."

"Are we getting caught up in meaningless nonsense!" exclaimed the lawyer Avram Levy in a commanding voice. This was the same Avram Levy who refused to protect members of his own family and thus his anger was expressed partly to cover for his own guilt. "All of this is talk, soup from a dead chicken, as they say. We must act; we, as leaders of a group of 60,000 people for whom we have responsibility, must act. Let's get to work! First, the lieutenant of the Grand Rabbinate along with you, Mr. Benoziglio, should again go to see Gonatas. This pogrom is not a joke! People are dead! People are sequestered, people are hurt, girls have been raped! The pogrom was not an insignificant event. Our delegation must act in the knowledge that in the future, Jews live in this faraway place so distant from the rest of the community. I said before that Camp Campbell was a place where such things could happen, but no one listened until now. And what do our deputies think? Why don't they speak up? Why do they stay quiet? They were voted in by the Jews, by their brothers, to do something, not just to take trips to Athens. They were elected for times such as these."

After further discussions between the deputies and Avram Levy, they succeeded in making a decision, and the decision was that His Eminence, the representative of the Grand Rabbinate, Haim Habib, along with the President Elie Benoziglio were commissioned to go to the Governor General, and after presenting our grievances and reminding the Governor General that what he promised wouldn't happen did happen, and seeing that the danger is urgent, to have the Governor General give the necessary orders to his assistants which would include:

> 1) First, to intervene with the anti-Semitic press, and to suppress that newspaper that pushes the people to the pogrom, and to suspend it.
> 2) Vote for funds so that the sequestered inhabitants can be relocated in buildings within the city, if possible in district 151, or in other places, but in the city.

After these measures were agreed to, Mr. Altabesh took the floor. He said: "It is regrettable that an occurrence such as this can happen in our day, but why do these events take place? Because we don't have the right people to represent us to the authorities! God forbid I should speak disrespectfully concerning the noble personality and holiness of our representative of the Grand Rabbinate, His Eminence Harbi Haim Habib. We do need a Grand Rabbi. But what kind of rabbi? We need a modern rabbi that knows how to adapt to situations as needed! For example the other week when we visited Governor Gonatas, Rabbi Harbi Haim wouldn't offer his hand to the Governor's wife and that seemed strange to us. When we later asked Rabbi Harbi Haim for an explanation, he told us that he couldn't offer his hand to a woman who might be on her period. How embarrassing! Most of all for the Jewish people. It's because of this kind of behavior that I see as an urgent and absolute need to find and bring to Salonika a capable leader to guide us.

Rabbi Harbi Haim Habib, 1930.

"Our world is being destroyed," Lawyer Avram Levy spoke in an impressive tone, "but, no! Many times, no! We cannot leave things as they stand. Furthermore, we can solve this problem of housing the poor! Abandon the settlements? No, a thousand times no!"

And so the meeting ended with a lot of commotion, and indignation. That is how things went the day after the pogrom.

*****

On Spinoza
(A Sephardic lesson)

A freethinker once said mockingly to Rabbi Pinchas, "Would you like to know what the philosopher Spinoza wrote in one of his works? He wrote that man in no way stands higher than an animal and that he has the same nature".

"Is that so" remarked the Rabbi, "Then how do you explain the fact that up until now the animals haven't produced a Spinoza?"

*****

When Mr. Benoziglio, Chancellor Daout Levy, and the community lawyer Mr. Yacoel were nominated as delegates to Gonatas, they rushed along in their cars to the Governor General's office, but did not find him there. They were told that His Excellency was indisposed and was at home. So the delegation also went to his house, but there they were also turned away due to the Governor General's indisposition. Gonatas did send word to the door, by way of his secretary, that he was not ignoring all of the events and that the delegation should calm itself since he would telephone Athens and receive instructions, but the Governor would not receive them.

The next day, 75% of the inhabitants of Camp Campbell had abandoned the settlement. They were settled in synagogues and in the schools, and if they had relatives, with their relatives.

The following day Gonatas received the communal delegation with great honor and many smiles. Throughout the conversation he said that on the night of the Campbell Pogrom, his orders were not carried out, and that he would punish those who did not obey an order and he would make an example of them. He ordered that the Chief of Police, Calo Christianolis, be kept in constant contact with the Jewish community so that he could be up-to-date on all that was happening and how things were unfolding. In any case, between "he told you and he told me," not a single question was definitively solved. It was all a bluff and a tragicomic joke played out at the expense of the poor inhabitants of the settlements and the Jewish community in Salonika.

*****

The Sweating Villain
(A Sephardic lesson)

The town miser, who had never given a penny in his life to the poor, fell gravely ill. He was racked with fever, but he could not perspire. It was absolutely necessary for him to perspire if he was to live, and so the doctor tried by all homeopathic means to induce him to sweat but to no avail.

Frightened, the miser called for the Rabbi. He confessed and drew up a will in which he left a large sum for charity. "Write it down, Rabbi! Write it down!" he cried, "It's for the good of my soul!"

The Rabbi wrote down everything the miser told him, when suddenly the miser gave an unearthly cry "Hold on Rabbi, I'm sweating!"

*****

Many of the families from Camp Campbell were settled one on top of the other in the matzah factory that was in the middle of Vas Hralin Street next to the Flores chocolate factory building. An older policeman, a really tough guy, who was nicknamed 'Crazy Yavo' (it was a misnomer), guarded the factory. All of the poor who didn't have anywhere else to go were packed into that place like sardines.

Abraham the teacher, who was treated at Hirsch Hospital, had healed completely. He bore only a few scars from the rods, but still had not eaten a descent meal since the night of terror.

His wife Rachel spent the day running back and forth, to the cousin's houses, and all their other relatives, in order to have roof over her family's heads, but it was all in vain. None of their cousins so much as turned their faces in their direction. Even Avram Levy the lawyer, for all his fiery words in the council, still refused to help. Rachel finally found a hole-in-the-wall place in a hallway of a synagogue in Settlement 151.

Chapter 6: The Appointment of Chief Rabbi Koretz
Cavallo malditcho, se arelumbra el pello.
(Damned horse, yet such a shiny coat.)
- Sephardic Proverb

In 1931, once the complaints about the reverend and esteemed Rabbi Harbi Haim Habib surfaced publicly, Mr. Isaac Altabesh was given the responsibility for overseeing the final decision about Rabbi Haim, and, if the decision was made to find a new Chief Rabbi, then he was authorized to lead that search and find the right person.

The communal council of that time, with President Benoziglio at its head, organized an urgent meeting of all the powerful heads in the Great Zionist Circle. They considered bringing in a new rabbi, a model European, a great rabbi that would know how to lead his people, be it in good times or in critical moments.

Everyone was allowed to enter an opinion, and there were many opinions: Harbi Haim didn't shake the officials' hands, he wasn't seen in a positive way by the Greek authorities, he was too old-fashioned in his theology, he this and he that! The discussions were such a tangled mess, but a consensus emerged within the Zionist faction, the majority faction in Salonika, that all the negative things happening to the Jewish community of Salonika were because we didn't have the right person to represent us.

Still, there was no overall consensus when suddenly the Zionists raised hell and removed the leftists and the assimilationists from the discussion and only the Zionists remained. *(continued Page 70)*

1. Isaac Amarillo, influential member of the Community Council. 2. Rabbi Haim Habib, previous Grand Rabbi. 3. Rabbi Dr. Tzvi Hirsch Koretz, current Grand Rabbi. 4. Baruch Ben Jacob, Hebrew scholar. 5. Rabbi Jacob Habib, Beth Dine. 6. Rabbi Mordechai Beraha, Chief Rabbi Beth Dine. 7. Michael Molho, author. (1931)

1. Albert Molho, author. 2. Acher Mallah, Attorney, Zionist leader, Senator, member of the Community Council. 3. Mentech Ben-santchi, militant Zionist, Deputy of the Greek Parliament, died in Poland. 4. Rabbi David Saltiel, Beth Dine, died in Poland. 5. Ellie Attas, Editor of the French language daily, L'Independence. 6. Ellie Beneziglio, President of the Community Council. 7. Rabbi Haim Habib, previous Grand Rabbi. 8. David Florentin, talent agent, Zionist leader. 9. Colo Christianalis, Head of the Salonika Police Department. 10. Dr. M. Bourla, Director of the Baron Hirsch Hospital, died in Poland. 11. Elia Frances, Editor of the La-dino daily, Accion, died in Poland. (1932)

Their leaders unanimously appointed Isaac Altabesh to travel to Berlin (since that city was where the most important yeshivas in Europe were located) and bring home a new candidate for Chief Rabbi.

Altabesh returned and with great pomp introduced Dr. Tzvi Hirsch Koretz, a relatively young and inexperienced man, to serve as the Chief Rabbi of the very old Jewish community of Salonika.

Koretz, a cunning man, took all of the Salonika factions into consideration and then he made a magnificent speech that he delivered in the Beth Shaul Synagogue. He succeeded in enchanting the crowd, and the council was so enthusiastic about Koretz that it didn't wait for the contract to be settled, and immediately confirmed Koretz as the new Chief Rabbi.

Koretz was a very intelligent man, who, with his background and education in the best German schools, and his strong personality, usually succeeded in imposing his will on others. Before long, most of the Jews in Salonika feared him and no one was able to confront him.

When Koretz was appointed, there was no intention that he involve himself in the community's administrative questions; he was only to involve himself in religious matters. Interestingly, it soon became apparent that he actually knew little about worship nor was he well versed about rabbinical matters. Many times he was seen consulting with Harbi Haim Habib about religious questions, but since, as Chief Rabbi, he was, in effect, a religious dictator, he imposed himself on religious questions by force just as he did in all matters both secular and religious.

For example, concerning the rehitzah—the ritual washing of the niftar, the deceased—Koretz introduced a modification that was criticized by Rabbi Haim Habib. Koretz opposed the washing of the insides of the niftar on the grounds that it was unhygienic for the morticians that were obliged to carry out this work. But the rehitzah was—and is—sacred for the Jewish population because the niftar should go forth clean from the earth.

And then there was the issue of the hand-shaking. As noted earlier, when there was a visit from the council by the Greek authorities and it was necessary that the Chief Rabbi attend, Rabbi Haim Habib always refused to take the hand of the wife of the Governor General's or the King's wife because she could be 'tainted.' But Koretz, because of his modern way of thinking, didn't hesitate at all in giving women his hand, since, as he said, these old traditions were little things and thus without importance for him, but for Harbi Haim Habib, they were of great importance.

*****

The Laying on of Hands
(A Sephardic Lesson)

A pretty young woman came to the Rabbi.

"Bless me Rabbi," she implored.

The Rabbi spread out his hands over her head and blessed her, but he took care not to touch her head while doing so.

"Why don't you place your hands on my head?" she asked in surprise. "Blessings from a distance aren't as fruitful as blessing from near."

"How do you light the candles on Friday night?" asked the Rabbi. "Do you recite the prayer with your hands touching the flame?"

"Of course not. I'd only burn my hands!" answered the young woman.

"Believe me it's no different with me!" said the Rabbi smiling. "Were I to lay my hands on your head, I might also burn them!"

*****

As a result of these and various other 'modifications' to traditional rituals, there was always a great degree of discomfort between Koretz and Haim Habib, an uneasiness that could never be pacified. But it must also be said that it was precisely because of these differences that Koretz was appointed.

As time passed, there were continuing conflicts over their different approaches to religious law. For example, one day the wife of a brute and habitually drunk guard of the Jewish cemetery appeared before the court, complaining about her husband's conduct. With cries and supplication, she asked that the High Rabbinate grant her a divorce. So, Harbi Haim Habib, using as his basis for judgment the traditional argument that rabbis don't judge from the testimony of only one disputant, had the husband called in, and the husband did appear. Naturally the rabbinate also brought Koretz into this trial. After lengthy discussions, Koretz was of the opinion that the divorce should be granted, but the rabbis and Harbi Haim Habib were against granting it. Koretz then left the room as a sign of protest, and so the rabbis took the initiative.

The Religious Court then had the husband take off his shoes, and put them on backwards. The husband then told them, "Esteemed rabbis, shoes shouldn't be worn backwards." The rabbis responded, "Eh, fine, my son, since shoes can't be worn backwards, neither can what you want to do, be done. My son, turn away from your drinking and your brutality and be normal. In this way the All Powerful will give you good will, and even the possibility to have children."

And so it was that the brutal man repented, and the marriage was not undone unlike it would have been if they had followed Koretz' advice.

In most of the disputes brought before the High Rabbinate, Koretz was in disagreement with the other rabbis, but he kept his opinions to himself, and never actually spoke with the Religious Court or Haim Habib. Because he was a very intelligent man, he allowed all of the decisions made by the others under his care to be proclaimed as examples of the 'wisdom of Koretz', and so the community leaders viewed, with great admiration, the decisions taken by the High Rabbinate under Koretz and as examples of his knowledge and wisdom in all the areas of religious law rather than the wisdom and knowledge of the other rabbis who actually knew the traditions and the customs of the Jews of Salonika.

So the community council, reviewing these judgments that appeared to be the equal of King Solomon, granted great power to

Koretz; and Koretz, seeing the mentality of the leaders and their naiveté, began to make ever greater demands on the community. 4,000 drachmas were unanimously voted every month for Koretz' basic salary. He was provided with a full-time assistant, Peppo Ascher, an old worn-out merchant, who was placed at his disposal from morning until night. Koretz asked for, and was provided with, a woman to act as a servant in his house, and, in addition, a female attendant for his wife. He was provided with a six-room apartment where he lived free of charge. All-in-all, he was costing the community 30,000 drachmas per month when a common worker was paid 2,000 drachmas per month, and a rabbi 4,000 drachmas per month, a community teacher 2,500, and a Jewish community school director 5,000 drachmas.

When Koretz arrived, he spoke no modern Greek although his classical education had provided him with a knowledge of ancient Greek. Mr. Avram, director of the Regie community school, was charged with teaching Koretz modern Greek which, it must be said, because of his high intelligence and great persistence, he learned perfectly in two years. He then began making speeches in the Beth Shaul Synagogue in the Greek language when the King or the Prime Minister came to visit the community. These speeches and his facility with the Greek language earned Koretz enormous respect and trust from the community leaders, who naively said, "Thank God he has taken on these duties and this role for now incidents such as the Campbell pogrom will never be repeated," as if Koretz were the Messiah. He came to be viewed as so important that his demands and his orders were often carried out without them even being brought before a council meeting. Everything he wanted was given. He was the spoiled child of the Salonikan community, when a third of our brothers didn't even have enough to eat.

*****

The Rabbi and the Shamash
(A Sephardic story)

The city of Salonika, always renowned for its culture and its two great yeshivot that made for the glory of Judaism, would draw many visitors from all parts of the world who came to ask advice on a number of points of view from the rabbis of a certain yeshiva in Salonika. There was religion there, but not like the religious from Poland, where one was more superstitious than religious. In Salonika, they were purely religious—based on the life of the Sephardic Jew.

One day, the community of a great city in Europe urgently arrived at the yeshiva of Salonika in order to find the most intelligent rabbi. As it happened, the great rabbi was considered the most intelligent rabbi of the yeshiva, so it was determined, against his wishes, that he be named to the position of rabbi for this great European city.

Now when the rabbi was ready to leave, he summoned his shamash who was to travel with him. On the road, the shamash said to the rabbi, "Rabbi, I want you to do a big favor for me. I never had the satisfaction of being a rabbi. I want you to give me your position, and we will change roles."

"What?" responded the rabbi. "You didn't attend the yeshiva nor were you my student. What if you are asked religious questions, what will you say?"

"I will send them to you for an answer."

"Oh, okay then," said the rabbi who didn't really want the position anyway.

In the meantime, the crowds waited anxiously in the temple of the great European city for the arrival of their new rabbi. When the rabbi arrived with the shamash amongst the crowds, the two kept themselves apart from one another.

The next day, in the tradition of that city, the rabbi was invited to the temple, where he was going to give a speech, and the townspeople would then ask him to resolve various religious questions.

Since the rabbi and the shamash had changed roles, it was the shamash who was applauded for his marvelous speech, and the true rabbi who feared the humiliation his shamash would suffer, but he kept quiet. At a given moment, the president of the community asked various religious questions, and the shamash responded while playing the part of the rabbi, by saying to the president, "This question that you are asking me, is so easy to respond to and so easily explained, that my shamash (who was the true rabbi) will answer you."

The shamash (the true rabbi) responded to all of the questions, and the president and his colleagues were going crazy because the shamash responded to all of their complicated questions so easily.

So the true shamash became the rabbi of the congregation in the great and famous European city, and the real rabbi returned to Salonika where he wanted to be all along.

*****

Despite the Great 1917 Fire, the continuing Zionist migration to Palestine, the unfortunate appointment of Koretz and the increasing anti-Semitism among certain Greek nationalist elements, the Jewish community of Salonika in the mid-1930s, still contained over 55,000 Jewish souls living in various districts within, and close by, the city of Thessaloniki. The Regie district was made up of 1,400 families; the district of those left homeless after the fire of 1917, Agia Paraskev, consisted of more than 500 families; the Hirsch district, donated by the Baron Hirsch program for the Jews who were refugees from the pogroms in Russia, sheltered more than 600 Jewish families; Settlement 151, bought from the Italians by the dream of the great philanthropist Moses Merpurgo, sheltered more than 1,000 families; the Calamaria district, bought by the community, sheltered about 400 families; Quarter no. 6 sheltered 600 families; the Caragateles sheltered around 100 families; in district 12 around 50 families were sheltered. Campbell was closed after the pogrom, and most of the families were resettled in 151.

Each settlement had its communal school, with its teachers,

a synagogue, a Bikur Holim clinic—a charity medical clinic—a dining hall that gave free lunches to the poor students, and 'Torah and Crafts' (Torah Umelaha), a program that furnished books and notebooks for poor students. Salonika's settlements were truly models of community administration, and that is why Salonika was considered the 'mother to Israel' because it demonstrated how a contemporary religious civic community could be built and maintained.

*****

Richer than Rothchild or Baron Hirsch
(A brief Sephardic story)

"If I were Baron Hirsh" said a student, "I'd be richer than Hirsh"
"How would that be possible?" asked a friend
"Naturally," answered the student, "I'd do a little teaching on the side...."

*****

Everyone admired us! Our Greek compatriots always wanted to do business with Jews because they knew very well that in doing business with us they would benefit. We were an extraordinary community: we had the Hirsch Hospital donated by the Baroness Clara de Hirsch, rabbinical schools, the great Talmud Torah, three yeshivas, lawyers, chanters, butchers, circumcisers, historians, writers, philosophers, three newspapers in Ladino—our Judeo-Spanish language—*La Prensa*, *El Tiempo*, and *La Verdad*; three newspapers in French, *Progrés* in the morning, and *Opinion* and *Indépendant* in the afternoon; two humorous papers in Ladino, *Rizas* and *Rayo*; and we had four deputies and two senators in the Greek legislature.

At different times and in various administrations, the vice-mayor of Salonika was Jewish. In addition to the community-supported schools, there were the private schools Altchesh and Gattegno,

Pinto, Warsaw, and Attias. The Jewish community was also comprised of: three grand exemplary speakers—Mr. Baruch Ben Yaakov, Tazartes, and Merkado Kovo; poets like Hananel Hassid—director of the community school from the Baron Hirsch program; scribes like Mercado Kovo and Joseph Nehamas; renowned scholars like Joseph Hjia; and numerous Greek-language poets. These and so many others were the glory of the Salonika community.

Chapter 7: A Sad Preface Before Extermination

Onde ay la rasa humana?
(Where is the human race?)
- Sephardic Proverb

Who could have believed that such a community as Salonika could be completely destroyed, extinguished, obliterated? Perhaps we should have known. Perhaps we had forgotten Ahashveros, the powerful king of Persia, who had 127 nations under his rule. It is said he condoned the extermination of thousands of men, women, children, and old people in only one day because the Jews were fed up with this useless king. But, thanks to the wisdom and actions of Queen Esther and her uncle Mordecai, the Jews of that time were saved from extermination. That is why we Jews celebrate the holiday of Purim so that such horrors will never be erased from our memory, no matter how many generations pass, but even so had we, because we had been saved, forgotten?

Then, there was the Inquisition under the priest Torquemada, may his name be cursed, when more than 5,000 Jews were killed. How could we Sephardic Jews forget? Did we think such terror was only in our history?

Moreover, there were the pogroms of Eastern and Central Europe where over the years 15-20 thousand of our brothers died or were massacred. Were these atrocities not remembered?

But all of these previous terrors were insignificant compared to the abomination committed on behalf of a nation that was supposedly, in modern times, the most civilized of all. This horror was destined to become the embarrassing humiliation of the 20th century, a stain on the histories of all peoples, a blot on human existence. It is unimaginable that such an event could occur, so can we be forgiven for not imagining such a thing would come to pass?

Even when the lion is ravenously hungry, he eats one, two, three or even four lambs, becomes full, and leaves the rest to live. The tiger, the bloodiest of beasts, even when he is full goes and grabs the lambs and leaves many dead on the ground, yet doesn't kill them all. The Nazi beasts, however, never grew tired of killing; their goal was that of a blood curse.

It is impossible to write with great clarity about these crimes. No writer could be born who is able to write about these crimes in all the details. No one who did not experience life under the Nazis can truly write anything about the experience. Only those who lived under those beasts will know how to describe what it was like. The intellectuals that are under such agony about those events cannot speak for the millions who were massacred in the ovens at Birkenau, Mauthausen, Buchenwald, and Auschwitz.

I firstly accuse England that knew that there were crematoriums and that those crematoriums were being prepared to annihilate the Jews. They didn't even give warning, but indirectly helped everything to occur. England believed that the less Jews that were to remain in Europe, the better it would be for England.

I remember very well that in Auschwitz in 1943, shadowy Palestinians were guarding us Jews, and many of them spoke Hebrew. I had the occasion of speaking to them quietly and with a great deal of caution so I wouldn't be called out while working at my assigned tasks. All of these shady men said in unison that the British rulers of Jerusalem advised Hitler to exterminate the Jews so that one day they couldn't take over Palestine. You had to see and hear these Palestinian men. They wouldn't beat us, so the Germans, seeing their weakness, moved them from Auschwitz and sent them to the Russian front.

I also blame the leaders of the entire civilized world, even the Pope of Rome, for they could have done something, yet they didn't do anything. Why? Why didn't the Pope and Archbishop Damaskinos of Athens raise their voices upon seeing how tiny Greece fought valiantly and was then seized by the Germans? But, they didn't do anything. Couldn't England have blown up the crematoriums that were working non-stop for 24 hours a day? Every two hours in the crematoriums, one, two, three, and four trains arrived to deliver 5,000 people, 5,000 Jews, for burning. They were massacred. Why? Some accused the Jews of being communists and others of being capitalists. Some said, annihilate the Jews because they wanted to have their money, others said annihilate the Jews in order to have Palestine, and others said annihilate the Jews so that they pay for their wrongdoing unto Jesus.

Oh, what a crime, what an abominable crime! I am sure if Jesus were present during this killing, he would take his stick and he would punish those 'true' Christians involved in these despicable acts. Don't they say they believe in 'love your neighbor like yourself, and even your enemy you shall love?'

Much honor goes to the American Jews, and to America that put itself in harms way to save humanity from this agony. The American Jews did everything possible to save the most Jews possible, but they were thwarted at every turn in their efforts.

So, what is this tragic scene we will witness where the nations are committing such acts against the most unfortunate people in any era? I am certain God does not want this drama to begin. Why is this about to happen?

✶✶✶✶✶

Fighters and Strong Men
The Battle of the Warsaw Ghetto
By Myself (Semaya Abraham Levy)

The battle of the Warsaw Ghetto lasted for forty-two days and nights beginning on the first Seder night, April 19, 1943, and ending a week before Shavuot. On that first night, all of the forty thousand Jews still left in the ghetto after their wholesale deportation and massacre, went out to fight with real and makeshift weapons in their hands. Throughout the ghetto, fierce battles were fought for every house and on every floor of any building until by midnight on the forty-second day everything fell into the hands of the enemy. Only one four-story building stood in the ghetto as a fort from which fluttered the Israeli blue and white flag. The 'fort' held out against the final siege of the Nazis for eight hours.

Warsaw Ghetto, 1943

On the first Seder night, around midnight, German soldiers entered the ghetto and began throwing a cordon around a street from which they were to take away Jews as in previous mass deportations. Previously, the Germans had been accustomed to seeing Jews allow themselves to be led to slaughter without resistance, and a few dozen Nazi soldiers would be enough to carry out the deportation of thousands of Jews. But in Warsaw, in January 1943, the Jewish youth, mostly the Zionists, had already offered resistance, and many young Jews were killed.

So, in order to overwhelm the Jews, the Nazis on the first night of Passover arrived in six tanks. On reaching the main street, the Germans were met by an intense fusillade on all sides when the ghetto fighters opened fire on the Nazi tanks. The Nazis tried to flee but they did not leave the ghetto alive and died in the flames of their own exploded tanks. It was then that the signal was given for the general uprising in the ghetto. Jewish houses were covered with proclamations and announcements of the uprising in which the "Jews will fight to the last drop of blood".

The leaders went out into the streets and organized the fight. Every able-bodied man and woman was given weapons. The youth took up positions as sentinels on the street. The children were charged with the grave task of acting as messengers among the fighters in different streets. They were also to bring food to the fighters. The children performed their part in the uprising at the peril of their lives, often under a storm of bullets. The very few remaining old people, men and women, took over in the kitchens, preparing food for the fighters.

Everything was fully organized on the first night. Not a minute was to be lost. The situation was very grave. It was known that soon a fierce struggle would break out and it was necessary to be well prepared.

Early in the morning, a special detachment of fighters surrounded the German workshop where Jews were employed, and from the German arsenals, the Jews took the German uniforms which Jewish workers had been finishing or repairing. Special squads were formed of fighters wearing German uniforms. Jews also entered German stores and seized large transports of foodstuffs that they later distributed among the fighters in the ghetto. In the morning, the banners of revolt were hung from the windows. The Israeli and Polish flags waving side by side.

The ghetto appeared deserted and desolate, and no human being was to be seen on the streets. Everyone was in some building ready for battle. This time, when the German and Lithuanian police who came in as usual to supervise the Jewish workers in the German workshops, were not given a chance to leave. Soon all Warsaw knew that the ghetto had proclaimed a general uprising.

At noon of the first day of Passover, the ghetto became a battlefield, motorized military detachments, fully armed, appeared on the streets of Warsaw headed for the ghetto. Ten tanks were leading the procession of forces that brought in machine guns. By noontime, the first shots were heard and soon there was an enormous fusillade. Thick flames and smoke shot up from the ghetto and fires broke out on both sides. The battle was to last far into the night.

The Germans were now convinced that they were facing an organized rebellion of the entire ghetto that was ready to fight to the last person. The Nazis were fired on from every house in the ghetto that they tried to approach. Late in the evening, the Germans abandoned tanks and machine guns, which had been put out of commission. The gates of the ghetto were blown up. The houses on the outskirts were burned down after being vacated by the fighters. In the evening, an order was issued by the leaders of the uprising to cease firing. The surviving Germans were surrounded and taken prisoner. The battle-field was quiet, but flames and pillars of smoke were rising on all sides. The Jews were forbidden by their leaders to leave the houses and their defensive positions. The guard was reinforced.

Warsaw Ghetto, 1943

The next day, it be-came known throughout Warsaw that the German arsenals had been seized and blown up and that dozens of Gestapo agents had fallen into the hands of the Jews. Large transports of arms had se-cretly been brought into the ghetto some time earlier when the task of watching the ghetto was assigned to the Polish police who co-operated in preparing for the uprising. Bombs, machine-guns and anti-tank cannons hidden under potatoes had been brought in on hundreds of trucks sent in by a secret Polish military organization.

On the third night, the six thousand young Jewish workers of the so-called 'small ghetto' who worked for the German army, joined the revolt. Their position in comparison to that of the 40,000 in the large ghetto was a privileged one and they were in no danger of deporta-tion. But when they learned of the uprising, they set fire to their 'small ghetto' and went over to the fighters.

On the next day, 500 Jews dressed in German uniforms left the ghetto for the Pawiak Jail that was guarded by Germans. At night, the Jews opened fire. In the confusion of the dark, one could not tell which of the men in German uniform was a Jew and which was a German guard. The Jews entered the jail bringing with them German uniforms for the prisoners and then took the prisoners out in large groups as German soldiers. By morning they were all out of jail, and all of them, including the German deserters from the front lines, went over to the fighters in the ghetto, and were organized into separate detachments. The liberation of the Pawiak prisoners encouraged the fighters in the ghetto and evoked enthusiasm among the Polish youth in Warsaw as well as among those young Jews who were living outside the ghetto by virtue of their 'Aryan' documents.

After 40 days of fighting, it became known that instructions had come from Berlin to completely destroy the ghetto. Large detachments of storm troopers arrived from Galicia and the Germans issued an ultimatum to the Jews. There were a large number of German captives in the ghetto at the time, so the Jews replied that they were ready to give up the captured Germans on the condition that for each German prisoner, ten Jews were delivered by the Germans.

The next morning, the Germans opened the great battle. The ghetto was surrounded on all sides by tanks, canons, and other armament. The German tanks and cannon were showered by bullets and bombs from the houses and streets of the ghetto. A special 'suicide squad' of Jews broke through the lines and wrought ruin among the enemy. Disguised in German uniforms they crawled under the German tanks and blew them up with hand grenades, losing their own lives in the fires that killed the Germans.

When the final battle was over, a crash was heard, and the young Halutz hurled himself down from the top of a building, wrapped in the blue and white flag which he had guarded for forty-two days and nights. The flag was red with the blood of the martyr, the last fighter of the ghetto, who ended his life in this heroic manner.

The next morning the Germans triumphantly announced that the Warsaw Ghetto no longer existed. Thousands of German soldiers paid for that "victory" with their lives. The heroes of the ghetto fought and died like saintly martyrs.

Chapter 8: The Last Passover Before War
A la Guerra como a la Guerra.
(At the war, like the war.)
- Sephardic Proverb

I remember Tuesday, April 4, 1939. It was Passover, and we were preparing to celebrate the last Passover before war, although we did not know this was the case, did not know this was the last Passover our family would celebrate in peace and optimism.

I remember my father, Avram, a brave man, full of ardor and faith, eager for the future because he always believed things would be better. I was sitting at his side, as the eldest child of the family. On my father's other side was my mother, Rachel, a great woman, the daughter of a rabbi. At my mother's side was my younger sister, Djilda, and at my sister's side was my younger brother, Aaron. By Aaron's side was my cousin, also named Avram, an orphan we had raised as part of our family, and beside Avram was his younger sister Bella. At the other end of the table, facing my father, was my grandmother Oro, the mother of my father. Happiness and joy were upon us that evening, happiness and joy like we would never know again.

My father's two brothers were missing because they were military officers and serving in the reserves. His three other brothers were also missing given that they had wisely fled Salonika five years earlier and had already established themselves in America.

My father's faith was so strong that he believed there wasn't anything left for us to pray for. He always spoke with such pride

Semaya Levy's brothers, Sabetay (left) in Greek Army uniform, and Aaron. 1929

about his children, and how could he not talk about us? He was a simple carpenter who worked very hard for us to be able to study. His hard work made it possible for me to become a teacher and a rabbi. Aaron was still studying law at the university. An older brother, Sabetay, had finished school and had entered the army.

Djilda, the youngest one in the house, also studied in a community school. However, there were some differences between my mother and my father about what Djilda should become. My mom wanted my sister to become a tailor, but my father wanted her to become a dentist. They often worried about her.

"Avram," my mother said, "don't you know that it isn't worth it for girls to study so much. It will end in nothing and we'll end up buying her a machine so she can sew anyway."

"Let me do as I wish, Rachel," my father insisted, "I have no desire for my only daughter to suffer in life. If need be, we will go into debt, but we will end up loved for what we do."

My father always had high expectations for us, and, in general, every time my father raised his hat he would throw praise toward his children. When he cried, his tears were often those of happiness.

At that last Passover table, the Haggadah, the text of the Seder dinner, always gave us courage, and it also made me very happy to sing the *Vehi She'amda*:

> And it is this [covenant] that has stood for our Forefathers and us. For not just one enemy has stood against us to wipe us out. But in every generation there have been those who have stood against us to wipe us out, and the Holy One Blessed Be He saves us from their hands.

And I especially enjoyed myself when we sang *The Kavretiko*.

*****

Un Kavretiko
(The Ladino *Hag Gadya* with English translation.)

Un kavritiko ke lo merko mi padre
por dos levanim.

I vino el gato i se komio el kavretiko
ke lo merko mi padre
por dos levanim....

I vino el Santo Bendicho El,
i degoyo al malah amavet,
ke degoyo al shohet,
ke degoyo al buey,
ke se bevyo la agua,
ke amato el fuego,
ke kemo el palo,
ke aharvo el perro,
ke modryo el gato,
ke se komio el kavritiko,
ke lo merko mi padre,
por dos levanim.

A little goat which my father bought
for two white coins.

There came a cat which ate the goat
which my father bought
for two white coins.

And the Holy One Blessed Be He came
and slew the Angel of Death
who slew the ritual slaughterer
who slaughtered the ox
which drank the water
which put out the fire
which burned the stick
which hit the dog
which bit the cat
which ate the goat
which my father bought
for two white coins.

*****

My dear father was an angel. He was a man who never wronged anyone. On the same day when we were preparing the matzo, our neighborhood voted for my father as the leader of our little community. Our community formed committees that broke the poor into groups, and each group was given charity payments according to their degree of poverty. And in reality, there were many families that didn't even have enough for daily bread.

My father didn't make much money, yet our neighbors voted for him as their leader. To them, my father was a great man, partly because there were many times when he gave to others all that he had earned, and he came home with little money left for us. He was a Jew that really did what Jesus of Nazareth preached—he took upon himself the burden of the misery of the people around him. How often did he give of his meager earnings to those even poorer? How often did our family eat only one meal a day? That was my father, and he handed down this strength of character to his children.

We actually had very rich relatives who owned large houses and held large plots of land, but my father never asked for anything other than the one time when he sought safety for his family before the Campbell pogrom. And that help was refused. The rich relatives not only refused to spend time with their poor relatives, they would not help us morally or materially. However, during our Seder dinner in 1939, my father seemed to his family like a great prince, not a poor man at all, with his family by his side as he sang with such artistry and grace while he praised the Lord.

I worked as a teacher or rabbi in the community, but I was not working independently. I had obligations to create reports for the community, and I often acted as a bookkeeper for the residents. That was how I became involved in our efforts to care for those who were sequestered in our neighborhood after the horrors of the Campbell pogrom.

We had to deal with so many problems during those dark days. We had a very urgent mission to help people, and at the same time I was busy with the bookkeeping so I came into contact with almost everyone residing in the area. Roughly 30% were extremely poor, but they still paid small amounts to the administrators of the district. Some residents were, understandably, always late with their payments, but the council required that I remind them that they were obligated to make their payments. This was a job that, due to my own character inherited from my father, I couldn't carry out with any great zeal, but I did the bookkeeping perfectly and maintained honest records.

It pains me to write that not all of those employed by our community acted honorably during that time. The employees who engaged in mutually beneficial politics with the leaders were always promoted or received a higher monthly pay. I was never promoted because I stuck to my principles and refused to flatter others or change my way of thinking.

*****

The Donkey of Djoha
(A Sephardic Lesson)

Once there was a clever man thinking up original ideas whose name was Djoha. One day he decided to cut down on his donkey's feed a little each day. In this way, he thought the animal would get accustomed to eating less with the same work. Day after day, he was overjoyed to see that his donkey did well with less food. He decided he was a very smart man and was very proud of his discovery.

Then one day he placed an even heavier load on the donkey, and the donkey suddenly died!

"Ah, the miserable animal!" Djoha exclaimed, "Just when I had almost got him trained not to eat at all, the stupid animal died!"

*****

By 1939, The Zionist Party that brought Rabbi Koretz from Germany in 1933, wanted to send him back because Koretz wasn't making a good impression on the leaders. The leader of the Zionists, Isaac Altabesh, was at the peak of his power, and Koretz's position wasn't all that solid. He continued to live in an apartment of seven to eight rooms that the community paid for, and he continued to receive a monthly payment of 30,000 drachmas while the Prime Minister of Greece at that time was only paid 10,000 drachmas. However, Koretz had made a speech in August, in Athens, in favor of the dictator Metaxas, and as a result, he obtained the support of Metaxas. That was how he was able to maintain his power over the community.

Rabbi Harbi Haim Habib, on the other hand, who was the giver of very good advice, was given the title of the Grand Rabbi, but those in power did not take him seriously.

On October 26th, 1940, a special committee with Dr. Alevy as its head, organized a Jewish celebration, a Matanoth Laevionim, a special 'mitzvah' that usually only happened during Purim. Everyone who had money was urged to give charitably to at least two poor people, and as part of this fundraiser, various students from the community schools took part by reciting poems.

Our leaders also spoke. I remember the patriotic phrases that Isaac Cabeli, Dr Alevy's assistant, recited in a very dramatic manner. Cabeli was a blowhard and very ambitious, but those were the sorts of men who were able to gain power in those days. Many top military men and Metaxas himself attended our celebration so our leaders did their best to create a favorable impression.

Who could have conceived that only two days later, on the 28th of October, in the early morning, after an elaborate party at the German embassy, the Italian Ambassador, a man named Emmanuel Grazzi, would go to see Metaxas and demand Greece allow Italian forces to enter Greek territory or Greece and Italy would be at war.

The year before, in the summer of 1939, Italy had occupied Albania in order to create an Italian presence in the Balkans. The southernmost province of Albania, Albanian Epirus or North Epirus was a territory with historic links to Greek Epirus, South Epirus. In ancient times, all of Epirus and the nearby island of Corfu were Greek. The term, "Pyrrhic victory" (to win a battle but lose the war) comes from the Greek ruler of Epirus, Pyrrus who won victories against the Romans but eventually lost everything to the Roman Empire. Epirus was Roman, then Byzantine, then Ottoman until after World War I, when it was split between Albania in the north and Greece in the south. But it remained mostly Greek and the people spoke a Greek dialect.

When Metaxas heard what Grazzi demanded, he said, No! This was a very popular decision with Greeks, and that is why Greeks all over the world still celebrate October 28, Oxi Day, as an important holiday. But Metaxas' refusal brought WWII to Greece, and eventually, disaster for the Jews of Salonika.

In November, after Metaxas said no, Mussolini ordered the Italian army in Albania to invade Greece by marching from North Epirus into South Epirus. After the Italians invaded, the Greeks, including the Jews of Salonika, were very united. It was a true David and Goliath battle, with our vastly inferior numbers arrayed against the massive Italian forces.

The young men of our community decided that if we must take up arms and fight, then we would fight for justice.

In December of 1940, there was a great counteroffensive by the Greek army that not only retook South Epirus, the army was able to push back the Italians deep into Albania. At the end of that fighting, Greece controlled almost all of Epirus and they set up defensive positions in the north called the Metaxas Line.

However, all this was not yet known on that fateful morning of October 28, 1940, at 4:30 in the morning, when my father was getting out of his bed in order to pray. It was the custom the Jews to always begin the day with prayer, and since they needed a minyan (a quorum), the shamash came and awakened my father.

It had been an ominous night. The dogs, perhaps because they were hungry, made continual and frightening whimpers. Or did they have a premonition and were giving their hearts over to despair? There were no people on the empty streets, not even the villagers who usually came down into the city in their cars to sell their clothes in the squares. It was truly a night of entanglement and betrayal.

When my father returned home after praying, he awakened my mother, and she rose to make their coffee. "Today," said my father, "we offered a prayer that will hopefully be received. I hope today goes well and that work goes well as usual."

"And so it will!" exclaimed mother. "Don't wake up the children early. Let them sleep since they are tired."

At dawn, we heard the first warning whistles from the canaries in our Greek coal mine as rumors spread throughout the city. It felt like everyone's heart began to shake; we didn't know what to do with ourselves. My younger brother and my sister began to cry, and so I, of course, also began to tremble. It was the first time in my life that I felt such an alarm. My knees shook a great deal, and without wanting to, I sat down and tried to collect myself. My lips were dry, and then, like a bomb, the official news report fell on Salonika: ITALY DECLARES WAR!

"Oh dear God!" exclaimed my father. "Please take care of our children." He looked toward my mother. "When will these cursed wars end?" My father's blood ran cold since he already knew what war was like, and all the atrocious deeds that came with bloody conflict, but, war was upon us, and there was no remedy. So, in blessing us he said, "My children, you are going to fight until the last drop of your blood. You are going into combat, and we are going to overcome. We, as Jews have to fight more than non-Jews against this evil that has as its main goal the extermination of Jewish kind."

Although my father blessed all his children, he put his hand on my head, and on the head of Aaron, as well as Sabetay who was an officer in the reserves. My father proceeded to murmur various verses of the Bible, and my distressed mother went to his side. After each verse, she repeated, "Amen."

It was really a tragedy to see such a sad tableau, a father in fear for his children expressing the love of a father for his family, and mourning in anticipation the sorrows that were to come over them. There was war, and the war might come and take them all away. Tears fell from my parents' eyes, tears that only a father and mother could understand. I packed a bag, Aaron did the same, and Sabetay as well. I saluted my parents and kissed them, and then did the same with my neighbors who loved me so much. I also went to my friend's house to gain courage by going off together into the war. Aaron also went to a friend's house, but Sabetay went alone since he was already an officer and he already had his equipment stored with his battalion.

There was horrible chaos on the streets. Signs on the walls told young men where they should go to enlist, but most of us didn't know where to go. The new communities weren't military places, and we were living very far from the city itself.

You had to see the young Jews who enlisted singing and dancing. We sang, but we sang to make us feel courageous. Girlfriends kissed boyfriends. The married women and kids kissed their husbands and fathers, not knowing if they would ever see each other again. You had to see the old men and women bless their grandchildren.

And it is a great lie to say that Jews were unduly frightened. No, a thousand times no! The young men went off with their bags on their backs to combat the enemy. They already knew that the fate of the Greek nation was tied to their own fate. They had already made the calculation that if Hitler came to Greece, they would share the same fate that their brothers, who had been settled in Germany for centuries, had experienced. They also remembered the speech that Isaac Altabesh made at the Matanoth Laevionim, where he said that this modern day Haman (the Persian advisor to Xerxes who hatched a plot to kill all the Jews of ancient Persian) was determined to exterminate the Jewish people.

In fact, German consul in Salonika was already trying to have Isaac Altabesh arrested by the Greek police, but the arrest was prevented by brave Greeks who forced everyone to understand that Mr. Altabesh was defending a righteous cause for his people. For that moment, Hellenic justice prevailed and the government let Altabesh remain free.

*****

Judah Maccabee
(An Inspirational Story)

King Antiochus IV was a Greek king of the Seleucid Empire but he was a very bad and uncaring king. He ruled over the land of Syria with a heavy hand, and the kings of many lands paid him yearly tribute. He built a monument to himself and founded a city named Antioch. But, like all the dictators the more he possessed, the more he wanted, and so he declared he would conquer the world.

So foolish was he that he called himself Θεὸς Ἐπιφανής, litterally, God Epiphanes but more accurately, "The Manifest God" because he wished that all men worship him as a deity. But the Jews had another name for him—Epimanes—The Mad One, a word play on Epiphanes.

It happened that in the 24th year of his reign (168 BC), 213 years after the rebuilding of the Temple, Antiochus turned his face toward

Jerusalem, and declared, "I can no longer endure the Jews that dwell in the land of Israel. I know that in their hearts they hate me and hope for my destruction. They are not like us. They do not sacrifice to our gods, therefore, I have sworn that I will bring them low and put the yoke upon their necks."

Antiochus then sent a great army against the Jews. They sacked Jerusalem, and they massacred the people because there was no one to stand against them. Whomever the Greek soldiers chose, they killed. They sold women and children in the slave markets and destroyed the houses and streets of the city and all the academies where learning was taught throughout land of the Jews. The Greeks also broke into the Temple and robbed it of its treasure.

Many Jews fled to Alexandria and others to Babylonia and Persia. Antiochus said to his generals "Abolish the Torah, punish with death all those who observe the Jewish traditions. I decree that they may no longer circumcise their male infants, nor may they observe any other Jewish laws or traditions. Compel them to violate the Sabbath, to bow before our gods and bringing their sacrifices upon our altars and send my servants throughout the land to see that this is done."

The generals did as Antiochus told them. They went throughout the entire land of Israel, and they pulled down the synagogues and the Houses of Study. They defiled and destroyed the Torah scrolls and slew all who murmured against them, and there were many martyrs who died like one widow, Hannah and her 7 children. Priests of Antiochus consecrated the Temple to their chief god Zeus, and they raised a great statue of him upon the altar in the sanctuary. In Zeus's honor they sacrificed a pig and sprinkled its unclean blood in the sanctuary and when the people of Israel heard of this they shuddered with horror. But they dared not speak aloud as their lives would be forfeit, so they fled Jerusalem in great numbers and Zion was a deserted city.

Now it chanced that Appelles, a Greek Official came to the village of Modin, not far from Jerusalem, to carry out the decree of Antiochus. He raised an altar to the Greek gods and commanded the Jews to sacrifice a pig upon it. Among those who gathered was Mattathias, an old priest of the Hasmonean Dynasty and his five sons,

Jochanan, Simeon, Judah, Eleazar and Jonathan. When Mattathias heard what abominations the Greeks wished the Jews to perform, he said to them "My brothers, let all the nations that are subject to Antiochus obey him if they choose, even to the extent of betraying the religion of their forefathers. But we swear, we shall not leave the path of our religion to go either to the right or to the left."

With these words, Mattathias smote Apelles the Greek and slew him. Then Mattathies cried "Take up arms! Whoever is for God and His holy law, let him follow me.

Mattathias and his five sons, along with many others fled into the hills. In the darkness, they would descend on the Greek garrisons and, although few in numbers and poorly armed, they slew many for they were fierce with the hatred of the enemy and aflame with a love for their people and God.

After Mattathias died, Judah became the leader of the army. So incredible was he in battle, so merciless in pursuit of the enemy, that the Jews called him Maccabee (Makabi which means 'Hammer' in the Aramaic language) for he struck at the Greeks mightily like a hammer blow upon blow.

When Antiochus heard of victory after victory by Judah Maccabee, he sent his army to punish the Jews, but the Maccabees decimated that army so Antiochus sent his most successful generals, Ptolemy, Nicanor, and Georgios with a Greek hord of twenty thousand foot soldiers and seven thousand horsemen, as well as many thousands of Syrian auxiliaries and they paused at the City of Emmaus which lies in the plain. They camped and waited to give battle to Maccabee. So confident were they of victory that they brought with them Phoenician slave merchants carrying chains with which to bind the captives.

When the Jews beheld the assembled hosts of the enemy, and saw how numerous they were compared to their own forces, they were struck with fear. Seeing this Judah said to them, "Terrible indeed is the might of the Greeks, but more terrible is the vengeance of God when He strikes at the wicked! Fear not the enemy even though they are many and we are few. Know that God is with us, even though we are weak and our righteous cause will triumph over their greater numbers. Therefore, gird your spirits and strength and your hearts and be men of valor.

"If there are any among you who are afraid, withdraw yourselves from the battlefield! Also, the newly married and those who have but recently acquired riches, let them depart for they will fight in a cowardly manner, being full of regret for what they have left behind."

When these were gone, Judah drew up his forces in the ancient order of battle of the Jews. Then he spoke to them as follows: "Brothers! Let us fight manfully for the liberty of our people and the honor of our Law. Should we lose the battle, we shall all be slain, and our wives and children will be sold into slavery. Therefore, we must be victorious. Thus we will regain the liberties our enemies have taken from us, and we will be restored to our blessed way of life. Fear not, for the God who led us out of bondage in Egypt will not abandon us!"

That night the Greek general Georges left the main part of his army at Emmaus and came with five thousand foot soldiers and one thousand horsemen to fall upon Judah in the darkness. But Judah learned of his plan. He felt he could deal better with the Greeks when their forces were divided. Therefore, Judah purposely left many fires burning in his camp in order to deceive and confuse Georgios, and then he and his army departed.

The Jews marched all night long, and arrived at Emmaus where the main Greek army was camped. Judah observed that the Greeks were well and skillfully fortified, and that their numbers were many times greater than his, for he had come with only three thousand men. But he took heart knowing that the Greeks were fast asleep and did not expect him to attack.

When the moment came to strike, Judah commanded the trumpeters to sound the call to battle. When the Greeks heard it they were astonished and dismayed for they were certain Geogios had destroyed the Jews. Judah and his men then fell upon the enemy who ran in confusion and terror. The Jewish forces slew three thousand of those that resisted them. The rest they pursued as far as Gidarah, Ashdod and Janiria.

Now Gorgios, who had gone in search of Judah and had not found him in his camp was exceedingly puzzled, so he hastened back to the

Greek camp at Emmaus. When he arrived there and saw what had happened, he and his men turned in fright and fled.

Yet, even after all the defeats inflicted on his armies, Antiochus would not give up his obsession with the Jews. The next year he sent another large army, forty thousand foot-soldiers, and five thousand horsemen under the Governor of Syria, Lysias and his best general, Ptolemy.

Judah met them in the hill country of Beth-Tsur. With only ten thousand men, Judah routed Ptolemy and slew a great multitude of Greeks.

Now Lysias was a prudent man. He observed the spirit of the Jews and realized that they would rather die than lose their liberty and worship any but their own God. He understood Judah inspired his army with a heroism and desperation that was more than human. Therefore Lysias gathered the remnants of his armies and returned to Antioch.

This time King Antiochus felt fear in his heart and he fled to the seaside provinces of his kingdom. But wherever he went the people rose up in revolt against him and mocked him saying "Coward, run-away!" Whereupon, Antiochus, out of humiliation, cast himself into the sea and was drowned.

Once the Greek armies left, Judah assembled the people in Jerusalem and said to them "Let us go up to the house of God and purify it for it has been wickedly profaned!"

After they had carefully purified the Temple and cast out all the false idols and their altars, they brought in the seven light, six branched, golden Menorah and the altar of incense. They also pulled down the altar for burnt offerings that had been profaned, and built a new one in its place.

And so, on the twenty-fifth day of the month of Kislev, Judah re-dedicated the Temple. He lit the lamps of the Menorah and offered incense and burnt offerings upon the altar. However, when they wished to light the lamps, they went in search of pure olive oil but they found none except one small vessel of unprofaned oil that had been closed with the seal of the high Priest in the ancient days of the prophet Samuel.

The vessel contained oil sufficient for only one day. Yet a miracle happened—the oil burned for eight days until new holy oil could be prepared. And in commemoration of the rededication of the Temple, Judah Maccabee decreed that on the twenty-fifth day of Kislev of each year, the Jews were to celebrate the Festival of Lights or Hanukkah. For eight days they were to burn lights during this period adding a new light each night and sing songs of praise (Hallel) to celebrate the Temple of Israel and the struggle for its freedom.

*****

It may be difficult for non-Jews familiar with the negative aspects of the Metaxas regime to understand, but the quasi-fascist dictatorships of Metaxas and later, after the war, that of Field Marshall Papagos, were not anti-Semitic. Truthfully speaking and without wanting to praise the Metaxas government, the Jewish people of Salonika experienced no hostility from the Metaxas regime. Some will consider me a partisan of that regime, but I would respond that the events speak for themselves and were as clear as the sun. During these right wing regimes, newspapers never attacked the Jews. Not only that, but many times our communal delegation went to ask for something at the forums, and those requests were almost always accepted. Those realities made the Jews of Salonika very favorable toward the war effort. And so, siblings, parents and children, in-laws, neighbors, everyone joined together in this sacred war effort to defend Greece.

And it isn't true that Jews were afraid to fight or that they were only war profiteers. From ancient times, Jews were primarily agrarian. Almost all the Bible refers to the agricultural life of the Jews. Ruth, Boaz, Abraham, Isaac, Jacob, all of them were agrarian. In the Zohar, the foundational work in the literature of Jewish mystical thought known as Kabbalah, the Jerusalmi Talmud and the Baveli (Babylonian or Baghdad) Talmud organized almost the entire life of Jews around religious and agrarian concerns. After the Diaspora, Jews became merchants and moneylenders because those were the only alternatives left to them after they were barred from other professions. But the Jewish 'soul' is agrarian, and the Jews were a poor people who only asked for bread and that their children were not forced to die young. And for those things, they would fight.

Chapter 9: The Greek-Italian War
Los italianos son brava jente, (ma) para la guerra non valen niente.
(The Italians are brave people but for the war they are worth nothing.)
- Sephardic Proverb

The first time I entered the battlefield, I met up with my younger brother, who was already involved in the fighting. We were in the mountains, and a frightening snowstorm arrived overnight covering the forests in a thick, white blanket.

My brother was in tears when he saw me, and he asked about our mother and father, our sister and the other relatives left in Salonika. I responded to his questions in a manner that encouraged him to believe that everything was going well, and that there were no bombings in Salonika. But that wasn't true. However, my evasions had the desired effect, and he calmed down.

Then he took a pistol out from under his coat and gave it to me. He told me we had to move immediately and with some urgency toward the front lines because there were bombs and artillery shells falling all around us. I discovered that another cousin of ours, Avram, was part of a detachment that a very proud, but irresponsible officer who wanted to go forward without having orders from the General in command, had marched into a disaster. There were many young Jews and Greeks killed by our own artillery. I won't speak more about that officer. It was a great tragedy.

The war, like all wars, created savages of the fighting men. I was in charge of contingent that gathered the wounded and tried to remove them from the battlefield. We brought together those severely wounded and took them to the surgeons in the field hospitals. Oftentimes the less wounded were obligated to go many kilometers by foot. In our army, a soldier had to be a good fighter, a good nurse, and a good walker. We couldn't make mistakes. A small mistake could cost a companion's life. And then we made a mistake.

One of the most horrendous nights that I have ever spent in my entire life, and that's saying a great deal considering what would happen to me in the coming years, was that dreadful night of a great many disasters. A soldier named George and I became separated from our unit. We were lost. We heard a wounded Italian soldier call for help in the gathering darkness. "Help, water, help!" he screamed. We were wandering in the deep snow, but we ran toward the voice. Because of our job to help the wounded, we had water and medicine, but George, my fellow soldier, held out his gun ready to kill the Italian. The terrified Italian pleaded, screaming for George not to kill him for he had a wife and children. The pleas shook George's soul because he too had kids.

George shed a tear and he put his gun at his side. Then held out the jar of water and gave it to the Italian. "Here, take it! Drink!" George yelled.

The mortally wounded soldier, after drinking the water, gave out one last cry, moaning, "Wretched Mussolini, foolish Greeks, wretched Mussolini, foolish Greeks." At that moment, he reached into his pocket and held up a photo in his hand. George looked at the photo. It was a picture of the soldier with his family—three children, his wife, and his mother in front of a house and a garden of vegetables and grape vines. The man managed a moment of happiness at the sight of his family and children. Then he died.

George sighed and said, "Oh this terrible war, what do we want from it? You impose such pain on us, you bastard Mussolini and your evil partner, Hitler."

I can honestly say George and I were completely lost. We didn't know where we were going. When night fell, we couldn't see anything except snow, more snow and the outlines of mountains against the night sky. We couldn't even see any houses in our area.

At one point we bumped into, and stepped upon, a body that let out a cry from the force of our boots on his stomach. That experience only added to our shuddering fear, and that night full of entanglements and betrayals fell over us in all its evil twists and turns.

When it was dawn, as the day cleared away the darkness, we ran into an Albanian (the Albanians were fighting with us against the Italians), and we tried to ask him, by pantomiming, to tell us where we were. He couldn't understand what we were asking, and he couldn't tell us anything anyway. We then asked him to give us a bit of water since we had given ours away to the dying Italian and we were so thirsty. He didn't appear to understand. Then such anger came upon George that he just couldn't stop himself. He took out his gun to scare the Albanian. It was only then that desperation and fear made the Albanian seem to understand. He reached into his bag and brought out a piece of bread, then he held out water and gave it to us.

We remained lost for two more days, but we walked night and day without resting. Then familiar sounds finally started to reach our ears. I turned to George and we both had smiles on our faces. We believed that we had finally found the path back to our unit. Our people were very close, and when we found them, we realized we had been wandering back and forth between the two front lines.

*****

Rabbi Tanbaum Is Thrown to the Lions
(A Sephardic Legend)

The Emperor once said, "Rabbi Tanbaum, let your people and mine become one nation."

"By your life, O Emperor, what a wonderful plan that is!" cried Rabbi Tanbaum. "But inasmuch as we Jews are already circumcised, we cannot turn heathen. For this reason let your people be circumcised and be like us."

"Well said," replied the Emperor ironically. "But he who beats an emperor in argument deserves to be thrown to the wild beasts."

So they throw Rabbi Tanbaum to the wild beasts, but the beasts did the rabbi no harm. All who witnessed this marveled at the miracle.

However, among them was a free-thinker who did not believe in miracles. So he derisively explained the incident in this manner, "The wild beasts aren't hungry. That's why they don't eat the Jew."

In order to test the truth of the free-thinker's words the Emperor cast the free-thinker to the wild beasts.

They devoured him forthwith.

*****

When we arrived in the Greek army camp, we found ourselves among a group of soldiers that had already taken part in a major battle. We presented ourselves to the colonel of the unit, and we gave him our report of what we had seen. When he asked us if we had noticed any unusual movement from the Italians, we responded that, in general, the area we had passed through was quiet and an eerie tranquility reigned over the new fallen snow.

The colonel said to us, "Good, my sons. Without doing anything heroic, you have become heroes. I will give notice to the leadership, and suggest that you be given medals of valor." We were curious to know why he praised us, and then we heard the colonel give an order to the telegraph operator, and the entire garrison moved into the area where we indicated that silence reigned. After two days we understood why we were heroes without knowing it. Two garrisons joined forces with the garrison already ahead of them, and later that day, we captured about 1,200 Italian prisoners while only suffering very small losses.

At the end of the week, the colonel gave polished silver medals to George and me, and, to George an extra 'bar', and a 'half bar' for me. Then we began marching again. Many of our people were silent on the journey. The battle was at its zenith, and because of the heavy snow, there were many dead soldiers who, at first, appeared alive to us. It is not until we were at their side that we were convinced they were dead and frozen. We saw one holding onto a tree and another sitting as if ready for combat. "Oh my Lord," I said to myself, "why am I experiencing these frightening events?" The sound of the artillery bombardments rang in my ears.

If Erich Maria Remarque, who wrote the famous war novel, "All Quiet On The Western Front" which I had the occasion to read, had been with us, he would have had many scenes to add to his book. How can we have such evil only to satisfy the ambitions of one madman? I never saw, I never experienced beautiful chapters such as those written by the prophet Joshua. David beating Goliath? Yes, for a while we were beating the Italians, but those Italians who abhor Mussolini, least want this war! But they can't do anything about it. They entered into the dance, and so now they must dance.

During those nights, we seldom slept. It would snow and then there would be rain showers. We could barely feel our hands. Our ears were beating like tambourines. The snot from our noses became little pieces of ice. At any given moment the silence of the night would be interrupted by strong winds blowing through the elm trees. The Italians thought the trees shaking in the wind were soldiers so they fired their guns randomly.

Those nights in the snow and rain were the worst we experienced during the entire duration of the two-month battle. Still, I cared for the wounded. Still I heard their whimpers and their crying. And I went with George to carry the wounded from the battlefield.

Suddenly, a most tragic even occurred. We came upon 25 dead soldiers who were killed by an exploding bomb. With the dead were a few who, purely by chance, had survived. They cried like children. They called out to us, "Doctor, save me!" One said, "I have two little kids." Another said, " I have three children and their mother awaits me."

We did what we could. We finished the last of our first aid supplies, and then we were forced to wait until the following morning for more supplies to arrive.

Among the dead we found my colleague, Moses Grotes. My dear friend and colleague was resting against the hillside with his mouth open and his eyes closed. It seemed as though he wanted to say something.

*****

Little Rachel
(A Sephardic Ballad)

Little Rachel at the window
A Turkish man passed by.
He tossed a golden lira.
And to the café she brought it.

A twenty cent piece, a lira,
A five cent piece, and a luain
She looked in her pockets
And found nothing for tobacco.

Where the carriages link
There is an idle wave
Young girls and boys
Dancing the "petit-pas."

Doduna, Doduna,
My moonlit face,
Open the door for me,
For it is raining.

I will open it for you,
My handsome young man
But I won't give you my hand,
If I don't know you.

Your relations
Did not come to mind
Now they have become
Fragile like glass.

What a handsome young man
Tall and delicate
A red brow
And blue eyes.

In this garden, I heard my mother
Rosio sing.

Rossi is not my mother.
Who is the Count Animal?
That wanted to laugh at me.
That wanted to make fun of me.

The Queen, being so Maltese,
Quickly sent my young man to be killed.

Don't kill me mother!
Don't send me to be killed!
I am a Count.

Mother who gave birth to Silvana,
What work remains for her?
The chest that would touch
That of Silvana will not be.

Chapter 10: The Blockade of the Regie District
Kien mal pensa, para si se lo pensa.
(He who thinks badly, harm will be unto him.)
- Sephardic Proverb

Around the beginning of World War II, the Jewish population of Salonika had dropped from the nearly 95,000 dynamic, thriving individuals who were living there before the Great Fire of 1917, to less than 55,000 desperate souls clinging to a way of life that was clearly threatened. Many of us did foresee what was coming, or at least there were many who listened to the warnings echoing through our history. The Great Fire itself, the rising Greek nationalist anti-Semitism, the deteriorating economy and the growing appeal of the Zionist movement all contributed to the desire that many Salonika Jews had to leave and start again elsewhere. For after all, what was one more move for a wandering Ladino Jew expelled from Spain 500 years earlier, or to be more precise, exiled from the Middle East over 2,000 years ago? Another change? Another country? Another life? Another chance? A small price to pay compared to what might happen if one stayed.

So why did the rest of us not go? We all had cousins, aunts, uncles, brothers and sisters in North America, in South America, in England and France, and in Palestine where the new land of Israel was already being developed from the barren dessert. What blinded us? For some, it was the conviction that we were Greek. For others, our attachment to the city, to family roots grown deep, to the cemetery filled with the names on stones meant to last forever; for many, it was the prospect of the effort and energy it would take to move on. But were any of those considerations really more valuable than life itself?

So we stayed. We stayed, and how could History or God or Fate possibly play a crueler joke on the Jews of Salonika than to decree that the more valiantly we struggled to stay, no matter how fiercely we fought against one enemy, and even how many victories we won against that enemy, that such stiff resistance and such glorious victories only sealed our fate against a far more cruel and ruthless foe?

We will never know if submission to the Italians might have allowed Greek Jews to have survived World War II. Looking back, it is certainly possible. But it would have taken the wisdom of King Solomon himself to have devised a clever strategy of submission, and anyway, the larger nation, the collective Greek people, would never have accepted humiliation and domination without a fight. And so Greeks fought the Italians only to have the Germans and Bulgarians take up the battle.

In the fall of 1940, the headstrong Benito Mussolini, without consulting his murderous ally, Adolf Hitler, invaded Greece— a nation Mussolini was confident the vastly larger Italian forces could easily defeat. As the Italians marched through Albania into northern Greece, Hitler was furious with the Italians for opening a front against Greece just as he was preparing to invade the Soviet Union. Then, during the winter of 1940-41, when the Greek forces were not only able to resist, but to push the Italians all the way back into Albania, Hitler was apoplectic. He not only belittled Mussolini's efforts, in early April, 1941, he ordered the German army to invade Greece by marching through Bulgaria, and by the end of April, the Germans had reached Athens and a few days later, the southern coast of Greece. Greece was theirs to do with as they wished.

As a result of these tragic events, Greece was divided into three occupied zones split among Italy, Germany and Bulgaria. Germany chose to control the most strategically important regions. One of the most important areas was the city of Thessaloniki. And so, we proud Jews of Salonika came under direct German occupation.

At first, we were promised that the dreaded Nuremburg Laws that would have stripped all Jews of citizenship, civil rights and freedom of movement would not be fully implemented, and they weren't. But the petty, and not so petty, harassment started immediately. Our Jewish press was shut down. Many of our larger homes and various Jewish community buildings were commandeered by the Germans, including our crown jewel, the Baron Hirsch Hospital. By the end of April, while the German army was mopping up the remaining Greek resistance in the south, there were already signs popping up across Thessaloniki that declared Jews were not permitted in cafés. In May, we Jews were forced to turn in our radios, presumably to keep us from listening to any news about the war or the occupation.

In the midst of all this impending doom, Chief Rabbi Koretz was consolidating his power and acting like a king from the Middle Ages. When he laughed, he wanted everyone to laugh. And when he was depressed, he wanted those around him to be depressed. When Koretz stood up, everyone stood up at once. When Koretz sat down, those of the council sat down. The rabbi said things and so what he said was how things would be. The council made certain his wishes were carried out. When the rabbi was angry, everyone was quiet. He said yes, and everyone at once said yes, beginning with the most powerful in the council and ending with the least important, all saluted Koretz' nobility.

Koretz didn't recognize either the Zionists who brought him to Salonika, nor the brothers of the B'nai B'rith who gave him so much power. Koretz looked like a true German. There were many who doubted whether he was a Jew or a German.

Ironically, when the barbaric Germans arrived in Salonika on April 4, 1941, Koretz found himself in Athens getting ready for Passover. It was there, in Athens, that the Germans captured him and the Gestapo threw him on a plane sent him off to a concentration camp outside of Vienna, and to be honest, there were many in our community who were not upset that he had been taken away from us. However, in January of 1942, a curious thing happened—Koretz was returned to Salonika and reinstated as the

Grand Rabbi.

During the winter of 1941-42, our situation deteriorated badly. The Nazi occupation devastated the Greek economy. There was famine all across Greece and we saw bodies of people who died from starvation and disease lying in the streets. Our family was reduced to eating one meal a day and there were rumors that dozens of Jews were dying every day throughout the city. To be fair, Greeks were dying as well.

There was devastation and destruction all around us. My brother Aaron reported that his friends, even non-Jewish leftists, communists and socialist were being rounded up and sent to prison camps in Poland and Germany. Mother and father were convinced that Aaron would be arrested as well, but for some reason he remained free and he was able to live with us although he seldom left the house.

In 1942, there were still no mass deportations of Jews, but everyone in the community knew of someone—relatives, friends, business associates—who had mysteriously disappeared or been conscripted to work in labor 'camps'. Then in the summer of 1942, all Jewish men between 18 and 45 were forced to gather in Salonika's town

The order for Jewish men between 18 and 45 to report for Hard Labor, 1942.

square and perform degrading physical exercises while the German soldiers surrounded us with loaded rifles. Afterwards thousands were ordered to join work gangs and construct roads to Katerini and Larissa. My friends Ziv and Aruh died by the end of that summer from the backbreaking work.

Some families were able to avoid the severe internal travel restrictions and escape from Salonika to live in the Italian zone where they were able to obtain documents allowing them to live under Italian occupation. In rare instances, there were Jews who were able to bribe the Italians and obtain Italian citizenship papers. Some Jewish veterans of the Italian war fled to the mountains of central Macedonia where they fought with newly formed Greek partisans in ELAS—the leftist guerilla fighters. But most of us remained in Salonika hoping against all hope that we would be delivered from our misery in a German defeat by the Allies. That defeat was to come, but not in time for us.

*****

The Futility of Reliance on Luck
(A Sephardic Anecdote)

In every epoch and century, the great intellects (rabbis) were always poor.

One day, a great intellect (a renowned rabbi) held a conference, and he had his assistants spread the word that it would be wonderful for the rich to attend so they could reap great benefits from helping the erudite. One very rich man was so inspired, he promised to the rabbi. "Come to my house tomorrow!" he told the great intellect. "I was excited by your conference and I learned that you are very poor, so I want to help you."

"May God bless you," exclaimed the rabbi.

The next day, the rabbi showed up at the rich man's palace and knocked on the door.

"Who is it?" said the servant girl.

"It is the rabbi!"

The servant told the rich man, who was at the door, and told her to tell the rabbi, "He has already left for the office."

So the girl told the rabbi, "He already went to the office."

"When will he return?" asked the rabbi.

"At noon," said the girl.

At noon the rabbi returned and knocked on the door.

"Tell that rabbi I am eating, and that I am not ready to meet with him," he said to his servant.

The girl went and told the poor rabbi, "Come in the evening, since he is eating now."

That evening, the rabbi returned again.

The rich man told his servant, "Tell him I am sleeping."

When the girl told the rabbi that the rich man was sleeping, the rabbi moaned to himself: "I come in the morning; they tell me that he already left. I come in the evening; they tell me that he is already sleeping. Oh, poor one am I, who was born without luck."

*****

In February, 1943, two Nazi specialists in deportation, Alois Brunner and Dieter Wisliceny were sent to Salonika to solve the 'Jewish problem.' They immediately applied the full force of the Nuremberg laws. We were all forced to wear the yellow stars, and a transit camp, the Baron Hirsch ghetto, was created next to a train station where the Death Trains were waiting.

Our Regie district, built to provide shelter to the Jewish victims who became homeless due to the great fire of 1917, was almost a kilometer away from the Baron Hirsch ghetto. It was the largest community compared to the other populous Jewish neighborhoods, containing almost 3,000 families, or 15,000 people. Almost 90% of the inhabitants were poor and day laborers and the other 10% were the rich ones. There were three synagogues, but during this time of distress, the inhabitants of the district didn't know what to do—listen to the rabbi or go into the streets.

On the evening when the ultimate evil descended upon us, it was almost dark, and the streets of the Regie district were deserted.

The silence was almost complete. We could only hear the footsteps of the Jewish police force on patrol, so that no Jew could escape.

In the Matanot Association (the Hebrew Free School Movement) center where the children were fed, there was some foot traffic as various officials came and went. Buenica Sarfati with Lina Trabut prepared the lists of children under 5-years-old for the Red Cross because there were rumors that the Red Cross would take care of the children. Mentesh Emmanuel, the director of the center, together with Alberto Camhi, while preparing the lists of the daily meals, were quietly discussing the direction that the district seemed to be taking, and thus, the fate of the school, as well as what the police seemed to be planning. The police, the Jewish police, were becoming increasingly dangerous because they were taking direct orders from the Nazi occupiers.

Suddenly, Joseph Ouziel broke into the building and began yelling, "Brothers! We are in great danger. Someone from the police station told me that tomorrow the Gestapo is going to move against us. If you go outside, you will see how many police are there. The organizing has already begun."

Ouziel went on to declare that he heard the district would be evacuated early in the morning, and he believed everything the man from the police station told him because there was no such thing as a 'fire without flames.'

One man responded that he had heard on good authority that there would be no more deportations to Poland.

Ouziel insisted that there would be.

Another man repeated what the Grand Rabbi Koretz had promised—that everything would be all right.

The group was sufficiently concerned that they immediately put together a delegation of residents in order to obtain more information from the leading people and from the Jewish police. The commission was made up of Peppo Ouziel, Ovadia Moel, Medina, Jacob Israel, Solomon Qinhas and others.

The delegation spoke to the authorities and said: "We come in the name of the residents of this district, to take into account the voices that surround us; and if they are speaking the truth, then we may be able to take the necessary measures."

The authorities responded: "You are safe in your homes, there is nothing to be worried about. Don't be alarmed or fret. Have confidence in Dr. Koretz. Didn't you read his speech? Didn't you read the community posters that urge us to have confidence? Therefore, don't worry, for nothing will happen. This commotion is just from those who see everything negatively."

After this consolation, the delegation returned and everyone, even Joseph Ouziel, went about pacifying their families and the other residents. However, most of the residents, believing the worst, prepared their bags and bundles of clothing, as well as coats for their children and shoes, in order to leave the district, one way or another.

Some residents tried to escape to the Syngrou District. Rumors spread. Panic increased. There was fear and trembling in every household. The entire district was turned upside-down overnight.

The residents only calmed down when an official representative of Koretz arrived and publicly sang to them a classic song that included the line, "Don't fret, nothing will happen…"

*****

The Conversion of the Jew
(A Sephardic Lesson)

One day the governor of Jerusalem called for a ceremony and invited the rabbi of the city, who was considered the most intellectual in the entire city (at that time Israel was under the British mandate). People of all ethnicities went to him to seek advice. In a moment of general happiness, the governor turned to the rabbi and says to him,

"Oh, Great Rabbi, how great would it be for all of humanity and above all, Jerusalem, if your eminence were to change religions and become Muslim."

The rabbi was stunned. He who was the representative of the community for so many years to change religions? "That is impossible," he says. "For one cannot convert to another religion simply to please you!

Everyone has a goal in his or her life. Let's not forget that all religions are good and that God is love and compassion."

Many years passed and the Great Rabbi, feeling his death approaching sent for the shamash to tell the governor that he wanted to see him with great urgency, for he was about to die and wanted to convert to Islam.

Learning of this, the governor came running with an assistant to convert the rabbi to Islam. The governor didn't oppose him but couldn't understand, for so much time he had begged the rabbi to change religions but he refused. And now, "How quickly people change religions," he exclaimed.

"I tell you," the rabbi responded, "I decided to change religions in these final moments of my life so that I may not only die a Jew, but so that I may also die a Muslim!"

*****

Then, after everyone had calmed down, it was around four o'clock in the morning, on a spring day so achingly beautiful that nature was determined to be in complete contradiction to the events that were occurring within the despairing district.

"You must know what is happening, brothers!" shouted the shamash, Tio (Uncle) Haim Cohen, who came to recite the atoning prayers with the Jews of the community. He was just about to call the rest of the Jews to prayer that morning, when he noticed there was an unusual abundance of Jewish police as well as Jewish guards surrounding the district, particularly before the entrance on Agia Paraskevi all the way to Prometheus and Monastirio Streets. He also saw four heavyset German officers giving out the orders to better organize a blockade of the residents.

"No," said Mentesh Emmanuel, director of the school, "I don't believe Tio Haim. Stay calm and remember the promises that have been made! It is not possible that this great district, which consists of more than 15,000 people, can be vacated without lengthy and detailed planning and at least an additional 1,000 guards."

But Tio Haim Cohen continued to warn us: "Do not trust them any longer! I do not lie. Go see for yourself, and you will be convinced. I am 90 years old and I have never spoken a lie. That is why they made me the shamash."

Things moved quickly. At 4:30 in the morning the barbaric,

beastly Germans gave the order to evacuate, implementing a tactic already used in Vienna. The moment the blockaders took their positions guarding the perimeter, the Jewish police, together with reinforcement from the other districts, used their batons to begin beating people to hurry them along.

It was a heart-rending tragedy to see a Jew beat his fellow Jew. One should not forget that many of these policemen, wanting to save their own lives (and believing they could do so), became faithful servants of the Germans to such a degree that they went about their despicable activity with enthusiasm and determination.

Tragic and emotional scenes occurred: Myriam Colchon, the herbalist, with her son Bension, who lost his two feet fighting in Albania, was beaten so badly that her crippled son retaliated. The father had declared and promised before he died that they would never go to Poland so Bension lifted his crutch and struck the head of the Jewish policeman who then struck him, and Bension was also left half dead.

In just one hour, almost the entire district was emptied, leaving only those with infectious diseases remaining. Within two days, the last of the residents were taken, including those who were wounded in the war against the Italians, to the infamous Baron Hirsch transfer station.

I note that the Hirsch District that had become the Hirsh ghetto, already held around 8,000 people, but with the additional 15,000 from Regie and another 4,000 from other districts, 27,000 people were crammed into 3.7 acres that had originally been designed as a space for 300 to 350 families.

And so Regie, the largest Jewish quarter in Salonika was left to the air and the sun, and residents from surrounding areas came and took whatever they wanted. The homeless also came down from the hills during the night for plunder. Gangs were formed to compete with each other to see who succeeded in accumulating the most treasure.

From time to time, police officers assigned to watch over the Jews' property chased some scavengers away, but truthfully, Regie looked like a killing ground where the enemy entered and slaughtered the residents. It was quite a sight to see looters with bottles of raki from the taverns wandering around aimlessly, completely drunk, shouting, "To the health of no one!"

It should be noted that there were some, very few, but some, like the low-level administrator Ninio Zanay, who put himself in danger to help those he could, bringing clothing and medicines to the cacophony that was the Baron Hirsch ghetto.

This was the time when the wicked tyrant and traitor Vital Hasson rose to power. Sickening and appalling events uncoiled from the man and his snakes that surrounded him. So many powers were granted to this ignorant man that he seemed like Abdul Hamid [the last corrupt sultan of the Ottoman Empire], killing or saving whomever he wanted. Hasson became so powerful that no one voluntarily showed themselves in his presence, not even the authorities, May God protect us! (And He didn't.)

The Germans always recruited similar people to be their collaborators.

If the tailor Vital Hasson had not existed at the top of the dung heap, the unemployed Jack Albala was ready to take over, and if Albala fell, Leon Topouz the rag picker would reign, and if not Topouz, then the photographer Albert Castro or the unemployed Yoel Groufter, wicked men all, would take over. I cannot believe, but must admit, that is only natural that out of the multitudes there will always be those people who are willing to kill their brother for power.

Hasson, reveling in the powers granted to him by the Germans, became ever more vicious and hatched dreadful plots along with his advisors and attorneys. He even acquired a car stolen from some poor Jew, and a chauffeur, Aruh, although Hasson mostly drove himself as he prowled the ghetto. Every day he proposed new ministers and nominated cruel supervisors to keep order and serve as executioners. He established a committee that was responsible for bringing him beautiful girls and married women. He also had merchants and dozens of clerks to restock his headquarters in a little two-story house located between Stavrou-Voutyra Street and Sapfous Street. It was there that Vital Hasson and his brother, Dino, had orgies. It was there that they sent out their vile orders and commands, and it was from there that Hasson would blow a trumpet that he received from a certain Romano that lived on Prometheus Street to signal his latest alert or pronouncement.

Vital Hasson, Jewish traitor and collaborator wih the Nazis. Brought to trial in 1947 by the Greek government and given the death penalty.

Hasson began the day by playing his trumpet as if he was holding a military ceremony. The Baron Hirsch ghetto became like a small mini-state inhabited by helpless citizens ruled by Satan. It had its own ministries—for food supplies, for hygiene, for housing, for cleaning, and above all, for the treasury. So many formerly good Jews, without thinking, believed they could be saved in this way, and they became loyal to another.

*****

The Holy Men
(A Sephardic Lesson)

A Rabbi wished to prove the honesty of his disciples so he asked them the following question: "What would you do if you found a large sum of money?"

"I give it back to the one who lost it, " said one disciple.

"I don't believe you! You're too glib with your answer," commented the Rabbi.

"I'd keep the money if no one saw me find it," said another disciple.

"You're frank, but wicked!" Snapped the Rabbi

"To be perfectly truthful with you, Rabbi," said a third disciple, "I'd be greatly tempted to keep it. In that case, I'd pray to God that He save me from evil and give me strength to resist it."

The Rabbi beamed and exclaimed "God preserve you! You are the man I'd trust."

*****

As our situation deteriorated, there were many meetings called within the community. One such meeting took place at Rabbi Haim Habib's ordinary little house where the men of the Jewish community were gathered before they were to meet with Dr. Kalmes, the head of the political office of the Gestapo in Thessaloniki. There were rumors that in this meeting there would be discussion about abolishing the edict that the Jews of Salonika would be transported to Poland.

"My dear rabbinical judges of Israel," said Rabbi Haim Habib, "the Gestapo has called for a joint meeting—an urgent session so we may deal with the future development of what will happen to us. But according to the palpable facts that the people experience every day, it turns out that these ferocious animals want to destroy us. They have already destroyed our cemetery that dates back to

The 'old' cemetery of Salonika dating from the 1500s.

ancient times. They don't allow us to ride on trams. They have put us in ghettos. Each day there is something new, and when Koretz calms things down by telling us one thing, the next day the opposite happens. In whom should we trust?

A recovered fragment of the tomb of Joseph ben Choib, born in Aragon, Spain and who died in Salonika, Greece, 1503.

"Many times we have asked the Greek government to protect us, but they haven't been successful in getting anything from the Germans. What can we do?

"Peace to the Lord of the universe," exclaimed the venerable Rabbi Haim Habib looking toward the heavens with his eyes. "A disaster has come upon us from the heavens; a huge mistake. You can say they committed a crime, those Zionists that brought us this modern Rabbi with his approach that is taking us to these depths.

"We shouldn't go to any place, nor should we be sent out like lambs to foreign lands! Koretz makes all things sound simple. He says in Germany they eat butter and white bread, and it is a lie that there is starvation. He says we are going to spend our time in peace in Krakow, and that a very well organized community there will take us in. Do I know what real interests Koretz has?

"Today I learned from the lawyer Avram Levy that Rabbi Koretz told him that we are going to be surprised, and we are going to Germany. Now, I don't trust anyone, not Koretz, nor the Germans, nor the communal leaders, and for that reason, I am not going anywhere."

The senseless destruction of the 'old' cemetery by the Nazis in 1942.

"Dear, Rabbi Haim Habib, we should take seriously the example they are making of you! The lies that each day that they bring against you when they take you before the religious court? They removed Sam Levy, of blessed memory, in the woods after they made him write a swastika on the skull of the deceased Rabbi Asher that was going into the pile of bones of our dead! There is nothing, Rabbi Haim, that we can do to stop their tactics towards us. All that we may give them will only mean that they want more, and they will not be satisfied until they exterminate us," Rabbi Avram said to his colleagues.

"We must face our judgment," Rabbi Isaac Hassid said in a low voice. "If you don't want to come to the meeting, we are still going to go. This time, it may be that the Almighty will take pity on us, and our blessed Lord will save us. Let's go, the time is already approaching, we are going to go, and you, Rabbi Avram, should leave behind your egotism.

"Will the transportations continue? Even if you aren't going to respond, you are going to just let us speak. Koretz, by the way, has already told us more than once that these people always speak little. Let's go brothers, with the help of God, we will succeed in convincing and taking them on the good path for us and naturally for the Jewish collectivity that remain."

"Rabbi Isaac, don't tell me this. Didn't they begin to beat us again with a whip? Don't you know that it is Koretz that is officially inviting us? Koretz is going to cause ruin to Salonikan Judaism and its history that dates back so many years. That is, he will do this in collaboration with his group," said Rabbi Haim Habib.

Rabbi Avram convinced Peppo Asher, Koretz's messenger to call the politopilacas—those whose job it was to accompany the rabbis to the community meeting.

At 10:00 at night, the communal meeting place located on Sarautaporos Street was ablaze with light. The administration of the Chief Rabbi continues to write lists for the Germans, and the writers all had sashes and many of them even had higher honors. Raphel Menashe, Harbi Haim's secretary, was putting the dossiers in order. Everything was already prepared. The large mirror, the painted chairs with the order of the Gestapo, the yellow V (for victory) at the entrance of the door, the black table, the paintings, the flowers, and the colors almost made us forget the tragedy—the Jewish tragedy.

It was around 10:30, when a caravan of three buses of German soldiers from the S.S, armed from head to toe, arrived in the garden between the community meeting place and the little rabbinical courthouse. They positioned their machine guns and their hand grenades. It really looked like they were on the brink of war. Aron Amar, the messenger for the community, upon seeing this collection of weapons, developed stomach cramps as he swayed back and forth.

Harbi Haim didn't lose courage. He spoke to Dr. Kalmes and told him, "We were invited. We did our duty and we came."

"How many of you came?" asked Kalmes.

"Three that are from the religious court and Dr. Koretz who is already here."

"Wait for me inside. I am going to put everything in order, and

I will return."

The commons was blocked by the soldiers with rifles in hand, steel helmets, machine guns, hand grenades and field glasses. They looked like devils in the shapes of humans.

Rabbi Isaac Hassid looked for Rabbi Avram and couldn't find him. Then, without any hesitation, he grabbed onto Koretz' messenger Peppo Acher, who looked like an important person, and, in this manner, the number that was agreed upon to attend the meeting was met.

"And if Kalmes meets Peppo? What will become of us?" said Harbi Haim

"It doesn't matter," said Koretz. "Kalmes is coming now, and I want you to be correct in your appearance, to speak little, and understand a lot."

When Dr. Kalmes returned, he immediately began his interrogation. "During Passover, why do they say that you put Christian blood on the matzah?"

"This topic about blood already cost us Jews a lot in the Middle Ages. I don't think that currently, in the 20th century, such nonsense should be repeated," answered Koretz.

Kalmes frowned. "Why don't you tell me now, rabbi, why you leave your beard so? Don't you know that it is anti-hygienic?"

"Any representative of a religion can be obligated to leave their beard unshaven. Can it be that your representatives of the religion that you say you believe in don't have beards?"

"We don't believe in Christ," said Kalmes. "Our Savior and the Savior of Humanity is the Fuhrer."

So, Kalmes gives a tug on Haim's beard, while murmuring different words in the German language, and then he points at Peppo with a sarcastic smile and shouts, "And him, why doesn't he have a beard?"

At that moment fear overcame Peppo the messenger. He turned red, and began to tremble. Then, Harbi Haim says to Kalmes, "This man is learning the books of the rabbinate."

Kalmes stared at Peppo. "If I don't mistake myself, are you not with Koretz?" asked Kalmes.

"Ko…Ko…retz?" stammered Peppo. "No, no! Not Koretz."

Kalmes, who looked like he had the face of a mouse, shouted, "You're lying!"

Kalmes then ordered the soldiers from the S.S to take the three 'rabbis' into the water closet of the building of the court house, and Kalmes violated Harbi Haim once again with a broomstick, while threatening the rabbi that he should say various prayers.

After that useless meeting and its aftermath, it became clear that Rabbi Harbi Haim was slowly being destroyed by the continual abuse and he couldn't put up with the disgrace and humiliation that was being forced upon him.

Dr. Koretz, on the other hand, remained optimistic. He saw everything in the best possible light since he lived with his family far from Hasson's inferno. There was also disagreement and arguing among some members of the council, and this continual dissention made the people believe that Koretz was playing with the lives of the community.

*****

The Rabbi and the Atheist
(A Sephardic Lesson)

An Atheist once came to see a wonder-working Rabbi. "Shalom Alechem, Rabbi".

"Alechem ashalom" answered the Rabbi.

The atheist took a guilden and handed it to the Rabbi.

The Rabbi pocketed it. "No doubt you've come to see me about something" he said, "maybe your wife is childless and you want me to pray for her?"

"No Rabbi, I'm not married" replied the atheist. Thereupon, he gave the Rabbi another guilden that the Rabbi pocketed.

"But there must be something you wish to ask me," said the Rabbi. "Possibly you've committed a sin and you'd like me to intercede with God for you?"

"No Rabbi, I don't know of any sin I've committed," and again he gave the Rabbi a guilden, and again the Rabbi pocketed it.

"Maybe business is bad and you want me to bless you?" asked the Rabbi.

"No Rabbi, this has been a prosperous year for me". Once more the atheist gave him a guilden.

"What do you want of me anyway?" asked the Rabbi a little perplexed.

"Nothing" replied the atheist, "I merely wished to see how long a man can go on taking money for nothing".

*****

Nazi collaborators and traitors, Jack Albala (l.) and Edgar Cougnio (r.), at their trial in 1947, when they were given the death penalty.

Then came the night when, at midnight, on March 19, 1943, a vehicle, driven by an Italian soldier, came and took the council's legal advisor, Yamtov Yacoel, and his family, along with many of the community's archives, and left for the capitol, Athens. There were also four English Jewish soldiers who escaped by putting themselves into coffins. The coffins were then carried by Daviro, a wedding assistant with Liao Alhanati, who brought them into Salonika from the cemetery at Zeitelik. From there, they also fled along with Yacoel.

In Athens, the situation was somewhat more tolerable than in Thessaloniki because the Italians, who administered Athens, were a bit more sensitive than the Germans. Furthermore, it was far more difficult to identify Jews who were not living in ghettoes from the other million inhabitants of that large city. However, in Athens, as in Salonika, there were no lack of spies.

Perhaps the English Jews were saved, I do not know, but Yacoel was eventually caught by chance in a house that the Germans had entered for other reasons, but they also found Yacoel. He was then beaten until he told them where his family could be found, and together with his family, Yacoel was sent to a concentration camp in Germany.

Yacoel and the English Jews' escape put Koretz in a predicament. The Germans, believing the information supplied by the traitor Albala, accused Koretz of knowing about the scheme and aiding Yacoel's escape. Koretz became so nervous that no one in the community could help him. It was curious to see that he also began to live in fear and no longer appeared so carefree and optimistic.

By the time of the escape of the English Jews and the legal advisor Yacoel, almost 75% of the residents of the Hirsch district had already been transported to Poland. This made life impossible. The residents of the other districts began to understand that Rabbi Habib was right, and that the community, Koretz, Hasson, and all the rest were only fighting to protect themselves, and all of the moving speeches and encouragements of the Chief Rabbi all went into thin air in light of the continuing, daily transportations.

There was one last desperate attempt to save the community. 107 Jewish merchants, intellectuals, and the council, proposed that 50% of the fixed communal fortune, plus 50% of all cash deposits were to be handed over to the Gestapo and the miserable Max Mertin, the German administrator of Salonika in order to stop the transportations and preserve the remaining community. This was agreed to by Mertin, and the commander in charge of the criminal Gestapo, Dieter Wisliceny, but when a memorandum of the agreement was reviewed in Berlin, it was seen to be too sympathetic to the Jews, and it was rejected.

And so the transportations continued and the hell that was the Hirsch ghetto remained in place. Some did what they could. Haim Emmanuel from Shivat-Sion (Return to Zion Association) worked at the ministry of residences, taking responsibility for sheltering people in places where the threat of transport to Poland was less likely. At the far end of Hirsch, near the dealer of wood supplies, he arranged for Madam Flor to have a quaint apartment on top of

Arditti's coffee shop on the same block where the traitor Topouz lived with his family. They also avoided, for a while, transportation.

Then there were also good Jews like Perez Trabut who did all that was possible to find other good Jews not in Hirsch like his cousins who came to the aid of the poor residents. Mr. Zacques Revah, Leon Moshe and Yules Naar made beyond-human sacrifices at the risk of everything to receive special authority from the head of the Gestapo to fill wagons with food, since the residents were starving. Haguel, Hanoca, and Uziel, were in charge of keeping the district clean. Bernard Landau, Zac Frances, Solomon Naz, and Mentesh Emmanuel were in charge of charity operations. Doctors Maissa, Elgava, Pesah, Samelica, and others were in charge of the hospital in order to provide medicine for the sick and to send them in as healthy a state as possible to Poland.

*****

Qualifications for Paradise
(A Sephardic Lesson)

The gate of Paradise stood open and the procession of the souls of men reached to the Heavenly Tribunal.

First came a Rabbi. "I'm learned in the Torah," he said. "Night and day I have poured over the word of God. I, therefore, deserve a place in Paradise."

"Just a moment" called out the Recording Angel. First, we must make an investigation. We've got to find out what was the motive for your study? Did you apply yourself to learning for its own sake? Was it for the sake of honor, or for mercenary reasons?"

Next came a saintly man. "How I fasted in the life I left behind! I observed all the six hundred and thirteen religious duties scrupulously. I bathed several times a day, and I studied the mysteries of the Zohar ceaselessly."

"Just a moment" cried the Recording Angel, "We first have to make our investigation about the purity of your intentions".

Then a tavern-keeper approached. He said simply "My door was always open to the homeless and I fed whoever was in need and hungry."

"Open the Gates of Paradise," cried the Recording Angel, "No investigation is needed".

*****

It is true that we residents were so tired of this life of agony that we prepared regularly and without protest to leave for Poland. We were starving. We were filthy. We were exhausted. Each day, Traitor Hasson posted on a wall outside the Hirsch station the names of those who would leave the following morning at four o'clock on the transport train. We were told we should hand over our money to the committee and receive checks for the bank of Poland. We were to hand over our precious jewels to the jackal Hasson. Whoever did not hand over their cash and jewels was to be shot on the spot.

To frighten the people, Hasson shot two young men who were about to escape the ghetto. He shot them in the courtyard of the insane asylum—the place where the Germans carried out executions. He did so in front of the rich of the district so that they would be so scared they would sign over all their property. There were some cases where people would tell Hasson that in such and such a place, such and such a gold dealer hid their property. Then Hasson would go to that place and take it all. Madam Flor surrendered all of her gold to Hasson. Terrified people gladly gave their Stars of David, their rings (except their wedding rings), earrings— anything made out of gold to avoid being shot.

During this time, Hasson's lady friends profited each and every day. Ms. Fifi, Ms. Bijou, Ms. Rachel, Ms. Solance, and others. Every night he had a new female friend. Food and drink were unobtainable during this time of starvation, yet Hasson possessed all he wanted in abundance.

It was common in this muddle of men, for members of commissions who were all powerful at one time, to ask for the release of their family members, but these men no longer controlled any wealth or power since their positions were already eliminated. Hasson no longer listened to anyone, and if some member of his party did not obey him, he would immediately take away their position and give it to someone else. And so our lives were lived under loathsome reign of this tyrant before we boarded the death trains for Poland.

*****

The Adventure
(A Sephardic Poem)

Unfortunate is my adventure.
Where you went to live,
In the dark street,
Where I cannot walk.

I once told you.
I will tell you again.
Due to a young man from Izmir,
for him I will die.

I already told you my dear lady,
If you want to conquer love,
Go to a house and burn the flames.
Fight with your... Lord.

At first sight I loved you.
I am yours for life.
In an oven I was disarmed,
like a fine plate.

Oh Bajo, believe me,
that in your weak visions,
you are wise. Cure me,
for my heart is in your lips.

You are wise, cure me.
Look at me so I don't get angry.
I saw a dead one struggle.
It is you that I must reach,
in the room or in the street.

Oh Bajo, believe me,
that in your weak visions,
you are wise. Cure me,
for my heart is in your lips.

*****

I cannot say my family lived in fear. We were beyond fear. I cannot say we lived in hope. We were beyond hope. Our mother Rachel was going blind, perhaps a blessing that she could not see what was happening to her family. Our father, Abraham gave up his food so that others could have a small bite to eat. He starved like so many others. Death was our daily companion.

And so we waited. Each day we checked the notice board to see if our names were posted for transport. Our dying father urged Aaron and Djilda and me to flee. We all refused. The family would stay together. We promised to stay together. "Maybe things will be better in Poland," said our mother Rachel. Even the rebellious Aaron did not have the heart to share our fears that things might even be worse.

What should we have done? What could we have done? We waited. The ghetto was deteriorating into a carnival of chaos and insanity. Hasson blew his trumpet. Each day more families boarded the trains and departed. Each day more Jews died of starvation. We were descending into Hell, and our God abandoned us to the madness and evil of Satan.

On a Wednesday or a Thursday, no a Wednesday, Hasson's trumpet sounded for us. Our names were on the list. The following morning we arrived at the Hirsch station. We boarded the trains. Our names were on the list, so we boarded the trains. We were a family. We stayed together, and we boarded the train together. We left Salonika together. Suppressing our suspicions, we silently boarded the trains.

Epilogue: After the Holocaust
De los mios kiero dizir ma non kiero oyir.
(To my people I want to speak, not listen.)
- Sephardic Proverb

Semaya Abraham Levy began to write this book about life in Salonika roughly ten years after he survived the death camp at Auschwitz-Birkenau, Poland. He collected Sephardic poems, lessons, stories, ballads, songs, sayings and proverbs, along with his own memories, and wrote them down because he feared that the Nazi annihilation of the Salonika Jewish community might also succeed in annihilating their unique, wonderful, and once powerful Ladino culture as well. This was in the 1950s, when virtually all of the notable commemorations of the horrors that devastated the Jewish communities of Europe were focused on the experiences of the Ashkenazy Jews of Germany, Poland, Russia, Ukraine, Romania, Hungary and other Central and Eastern European communities who spoke Yiddish and had their own rich cultural identity in literature, theater, art and song.

To a certain extent, Levy's fears were justified because the overwhelming preponderance of non-Jewish awareness of the fate of European Jewry is focused on the Ashkenazy experience, although there have been numerous significant documentaries and publications honoring and preserving the unique Salonika community. However, Ladino, as a spoken variation of Castilian Spanish is passing away, but then so is spoken Yiddish, as the years fade, and Hebrew is the chosen universal language of Israel, and Israel becomes the cultural identity for contemporary Jews.

Levy continued collecting and writing until the mid-1950s, and then his writing about Salonika stopped abruptly once he reached that terrifying moment when the last of the Salonika Jews boarded the transports departing from the train station in the Hirsch ghetto bound for what so many of them still hoped was temporary settlement in Krakow, Poland, and not to the reality—the extermination camps.

The Auschwitz-Birkenau crematorium at liberation, 1945.

He did, however, compose three memorial poems, two longer narrative poems and one short lyrical poem, which he clearly wrote from the perspective of one who survived the Holocaust, and which he intended to include in this book that he never finished.

*****

Those Without Graves

by Semaya Abraham Levy (1954)

31,500,000 old men and women, men at the height of their youth, women and children "without graves."
31,500,000 human beings...
31,500,000 innocent souls...
6,500,000 human beings, guilty of just one crime, that of being Jewish...
They died!
Slaughtered, shot, and suffocated...
They died!
Burned alive!

They died!
Suffocated in the crematoriums!
They died!
From hunger, from cold, and from exhaustion
in the Nazi extermination camps...
They died!
In the barracks of experience...
They died!
In the seats where their genital organs were removed...
They died!
"Without graves" without funereal marble, without tombs...
They died!
Burned like mice...
They died!
Twice, given that not even traces of their tombs remained, the first
part of these disappeared saints don't have anyone to cry for them...
They died!
Without those, who were lucky to remain alive, having a place to
mourn and cry for them!
Nothing!
The memory of this "abominable cry" does not carry on, where these atrocities were unequal to any other in human history!
Nothing!
There was no life, unless humanity becomes conscious of its responsibility for this ruthless atrocity...

Discarded bodies in Auschwitz-Birkenau at liberation, 1945.

Nothing!
May the coming generations be forewarned, so that they realize
what a barbaric state civilization can become if one does not take
precaution...
Nothing!
Certainly, may this serve as a lesson to those of the future so that
they are aware of the lamentable and barbaric state people can fall

into, all of humanity and civilization, if it does not take caution.

*****

Why Are There No Tombs?
by Semaya Abraham Levy (March 21, 1954)

My father! This man of high culture
simple and humble to any child
for his noble character, and his fine morality
was elected spokesman of a large city.

His principle goal was
to instill love and morality
in judging the helpless with compassion
and in helping the less fortunate with knowledge.

Love! Love! he said to every being
without making any distinction of one's race.
God! He created everyone in his own image
and everyone has the right to live in nature.

From the prophets and the spirits, may they be widespread
Brown, white, yellow, or red!
Moses, Jesus, Mohammed, or Buddha
that do not doubt anyone's existence.

For did they not advise love and kindness?
If not...society cannot prosper!
This was always the principle of my beloved father
who was supported by my dear mother...
Your heart would hurt, and it would enormously reach
the connection with the present, to that of my ancestors, the luck!
There! In the heart of this nation...archaic times
which organized the pogrom, the satanic approach
and the human beast, already becoming fierce and
spreading the most atrocious death!

Semaya Abraham Levy

The crematoriums, millions worked methodically
suffocating them and burning them, silently!
The killer! He did not make any distinction,
he killed and slew those from any nation.

Breastfeeding women! Old men and women without exception
found tragedy there...loss.
Everyone was burned in the terrestrial inferno,
in this horrible and gruesome torment.

Burning them! [...] They laughed, ah! The sadists,
a town guided by outlaws and social climbers!
No, my dear ancestors do not have graves,
like millions like them do not have graves!

Without remains! In ash, by the blowing wind,
and thrown in the current of the Vistula River
No funereal piece of marble carries the names
of millions of these sacred men.

Neither the poet nor the historian
nor wise scribe has yet to be born
who will write this terrible tragedy
that cost the height of our youth.

Similar criminals may not be born again
since these miserable people lack the knowledge
Oh my God, these people that gave us Mendelsohn, Bach, and
Strauss, also gave us the crematoriums... of Birkenau!

Sleep! Sleep in peace. dear grandparents,
No such bandits will pass by again!
Your names are already etched in our heart,
and they will be written with "blood" by our generation.

The Levy Family (l. to r.) Rachel, Semaya, Albert, Elvira. in Thessaloniki, Greece, 1955.

Hymn
to the Combatants of Warsaw.
by Semaya Abraham Levy

Let us raise the flag,
the flag of the nation
of the sons of Zion.
Together we will go to war.
Together we will die.
For the religion and for the nation.
And you, dear daughters
only daughters of the nation.
virgin and pure,
accomplished and fulfilled,
from you we hope for forgiveness.

You, my sons
the flower of Israel,
will fight in your nests
to save Israel.

Our nation is not lost
Israel is eternal.

*May our Father bless us
and save Israel.*

*Oh holy Lord, may we be able to
carry forth your memory,
dragged about in this horrible camp,
this extermination camp.*

*Oh holy and powerful Lord,
send us your recognition soon.*

*The modern Haman wants to destroy us
We don't see Mordechai, Esther, or Azuel.
The criminal wants to bury us.
May your name live, oh eternal one.*

*In the Warsaw Ghetto,
in your name and memory
we are in great agony
we wait for you holy God.*

*And you, representatives of God
Priest of Rome, and heads of state
Do something for the Jews
and release the people of Warsaw
You are God or you are not God
but you are the God of suffering.*

*Let us go! Let us go in the name of the holy God.
Let this classic song repeat in every generation
for the good and loved Jewish people
who abandoned the crucified Jesus,
the nation.*

*If you are truly Christians,
you should be brothers.*

You should save God's nation,
being that it gave us God's child.
Where is this religion that you believe in?
Where are the 10 commandments of the religion?
And your Jesus, come and see
what your representatives did with your faith.
You are God! Or you are not God,
but you are the God of suffering.

*****

After the Holocaust
by Semaya Abraham Levy (1954)

Those times passed by
when I would cry for you
now that you are burned
cry a little for me.

*****

We do not know why Levy stopped writing. We do not know why he never wrote a word about his experiences in Auschwitz-Birkenau. We do not know why he never wrote about his return to Thessaloniki where he married Elvira Schulhami on August, 9, 1946, and fathered a daughter, Rachel, born on August 10, 1947, named after his own mother, and a son, Albert, born April 3, 1954. We do not know why he never wrote about his decision to leave Thessaloniki and settle in Los Angeles, California. The only hint we have is in the following tale he 'collected' and probably altered to reflect his own sardonic view of fate:

It Pays To Be Ignorant
(A Sephardic lesson)

An immigrant came from Greece to Los Angeles. He had neither trade nor calling, and when he found that the streets of America were not lined with gold and the trees were not made green with dollars as he had been told in the old country, he became a peddler of needles and pins, and eye charm protectors.

Life was very hard, insults were many, and the profits were very small. So he kept his eyes open for something better when he heard that the job of shamash was available in his synagogue. He hurried to apply for the post. "Can you read and write English?" asked the president of the congregation.

"No" answered the immigrant.

"Sorry mister," replied the president, "in America a shamash has got to know how to read and write. L.A. is not Greece you know".

So the poor man sighed and went sadly away.

But in the course of time, the immigrant began to prosper. He turned to real estate and amassed a fortune. One day, when he needed a million dollars to finance a real estate venture, he went to his banker and asked for a loan. He got it instantly.

"Write your own check" said the President of the Bank, flatteringly handing him his pen.

"I can't write at all", stammered the realtor in embarrassment; "I've only learned to sign my name."

"Tsk-ssk, how wonderful" exclaimed the banker. "You have accomplished so much without knowing how to read or write, imagine what you would have been today if you did know how!"

"Sure!" muttered the realtor, "I would have been the shamash of my synagogue".

*****

However, Semaya Levy did not end up a rich real estate investor. He died in relative obscurity, much too young, at 62, on March 16, 1975, in Los Angeles, California.

Semaya's father, Abraham Levy, died in 1943, of starvation in Salonika, days before he would have been transported to Poland.

Semaya's mother, Rachel, and his sister, Djilda, were murdered in the crematoriums at Auschwitz-Birkenau in early 1944.

Semaya's brother Aaron was shot in Auschwitz-Birkenau in

1945, just two weeks before the camp was liberated.

Semaya's first wife, Gracia, was killed in Auschwitz-Birkenau in 1944.

Semaya's brother Sabetay avoided being transported to Auschwitz-Birkenau because he was fighting in the mountains, but there is no record of what did happen to him.

Gracia Levy , 1941.

Rabbi Haim Habib along with his wife, Hana, and one of his daughters, Mathilda, was murdered in Auschwitz-Birkenau in 1943.

In late 1943, Chief Rabbi Koretz was deported a second time, with his family, to the relatively less harsh work camp at Bergen-Belsen where he eventually caught typhus. He was then transferred '*with special privilege*' to a camp in Theresienstadt in what is now the Czech Republic. Three months after Theresienstadt was liberated by the Russians, Koretz died in Trebitz, Germany, a small village outside Dresden.

The traitor Vital Hasson and many of the other collaborators were also deported '*with special privilege*' to Bergen-Belsen. When they were returned to Thessaloniki after the war, there was outrage within the tiny surviving Jewish community. Hasson, Albala and many of the other collaborators were eventually tried and condemned to death by the Greek government in 1947.

98% of the 54,000 Jews alive in Salonika in the spring of 1943, either starved to death or were killed in the concentration camps. There are no tombs, no stones, no cemetery in Thessaloniki to record their deaths.

Appendix A

"Who would say that my head was a source of water and my eyes fountains of tears due to crying day and night for the misfortune of my people" [Jeremiah]

Semaya Abraham Levy compiled a list of those Salonika Jews that he knew survived various concentration camps and were returned to Salonika after the end of the war.

NAME	Tattoo	Name of Camp(s)/Date of Liberation
Abravanel, Dora		Bergen Belsen Feb 1944
Abravanel, Isidore		Bergen Belsen Feb 1944
Abravanel, Jeaques		Bergen Belsen Feb 1944
Abravanel, Sylvio		Bergen Belsen Feb 1944
Agapiadou, Marie	40725	Birkenau, Radisburg, Newstadt May 45
Aggelou, Olga	77030	Birkenau, Malhof, May 1945
Alcalay, Leon		
Alfandari, Oro	41581	Auschwitz, Newstade, Gleve May 1945
Allalouf, Bella	39966	Auschwitz, Malhof, Grimes May 45
Allalouf, Gabriel	111149	Birkenau, Auschwitz, Buchenwald April 45
Allalouf, Jean		Bergen Belsen Apr 1945
Allalouf, Levy	119795	Auschwitz Yavoshna-Behousen May 45
Allalouf, Mathilda	A8319	Birkenau Jan 45
Allalouf, Sabetai	115890	Auschwitz Buna Flosendburg May 45
Amar, Sylvia	41549	Auschwitz, Newstade, Gleve May 1945
Amarillio, Erica	38912	Auschwitz, Revansbrouk Malhof May 1945
Amir, Moshe	118441	Auschwitz, Birkenau, Mathauzen, Curzin April 45
Antzel, Albert	118494	Birkenau, Auschwitz, Dauchau-Mathausen May 45
Antzel, Leon	118493	Birkenau, Auschwitz, Dauchau-Mathausen May 45
Arditti, Rene		Bergen Belsen - Sept 1945
Arditti, Sarah		Bergen Belsen Feb 1944
Arouh, Peppo	115869	Auschwitz, Buna, Bergen Belzen Apr 1945
Attan, Mallah	109961	Birkenau, Warsaw, Dachau, Waldlager May 1945
Attan, Sarah	3619	Waldsdorf - Apr 1945
Attias, Esther	43053	Birkenau, Bergen Belsen May 45
Attias, Moechon	115918	Auschwitz, Koblenchase, Buna, Dachau June 45
Azaria, Mati	39295	Birkenau, Ravensbruk-Neustadt May 1945
Bahar, Joseph Moshe	116379	Birkenau, Auschwitz, Buna, Ebensee Apr 1945
Bahar, Sara	76912	Birkenau, Auschwitz-Leipsig Apr 1945
Barzilai, Ezra		Bergen Belsen
Beja, Claire	A8284	Birkenau, Bergen Belsen May 1945
Beja, Ovadia	122002	Birkenau, Flomaling, Buchenvald
Benforado, David	120743	Birkenau, Jawozno, Buchenwald - Grooersooen April 1945
Benforado, Sarica	44420	Birkenau, Auschwitz Jan 1945
Benmayor, Leon	119842	Auschwitz, Schwentohlowitz, Birkenau, Dachau April '45
Benoziglio, Eveline		Bergen Belsen Feb 1944
Benoziglio, Jeanne		Bergen Belsen Feb 1944

Names Without Tombs

Name	Number	Location/Date
Benoziglio, Reyna		Bergen Belsen Feb 1944
Benoziglio, Solomon		Bergen Belsen Feb 1944
Benrubi, David		Augsburg, May 1945
Benrubi, Mairy	39350	Birgenau, Auschwitz, Ravensburk, Par sayu 3 May '45
Benveniste, Mair		Bergen Belsen Apr 1944
Benvenisted, Lily		Bergen Belsen Feb 1944
Benvenistes, Julie		Bergen Belsen Apr 1944
Brudo, Moise	114964	Auschwitz, Buna, Warsaw, Waldpager May 1945
Burla, Rachel	44483	Birkenau, Auschwitz Malhof May 1945
Calderon, Daisy	40578	Birkenau, Neustadt March 1945
Camhi, Joseph		Bergmo, Bairo, Mouti March 1945
Capon, Sabetai	118575	Birkenau, Vanonzo Jan 1945
Castro, Filippe	119896	Auschwitz, Schenventoblowitz, Gouzim Apr 1945
Castro, Alber		Bergen Belsen Apr 1945
Castro, Fourtner		Bergen Belsen Apr 1945
Castro, Moise		Bergen Belsen Apr 1945
Castro, Plana		Bergen Belsen Apr 1945
Castro, Victoria	77077	Birkenau, Bergen Belsen Jan 1945
Chaban, Baruh	116619	Auschwitz, Warsow, Dachau, Kemferig Apr 1945
Choel, Jacob	116275	Auschwitz, Mathausen March 1945
Choel, Palomba	39965	Auschwitz, Bergen Belsen May 1945
Cohen, Albert	137001	Birkenau, Warsow, Dachau, Waldlager March 1945
Cohen, David	124387	Birkenau, Warsaw, Muldorf Apr 1945
Cohen, Eleanora	41579	Auschwitz, Malhof, Ravensbrook May 1945
Cohen, Estherina	76875	Birkenau, Bergen Belsen April 1945
Cohen, Eva	A8316	Birkenau, Auschwitz Jan 1945
Cohen, Germaine		Birkenau, Bergen Belsen March 1945
Cohen, Isac	119884	Auschwitz, Swentoblowitz, Mathausen May 1945
Cohen, Isac	115065	Auschwitz, Buna, Buchenwald March 1945
Cohen, Israel	116048	Auschwitz, Buna, Ebensee March 1945
Cohen, Jacob	120787	Birkenau, Auschwitz, Mathausen Jan 1945
Cohen, Joseph	182002	Auschwitz, Buna, Buchenwald Apr 1945
Cohen, Moise	109554	Auschwitz, Balitar, Dachau March 1945
Cohen, Rosa	40733	Birkenau, Nenstadt March 1945
Comfortez, Sam	116476	Mathausen, Kuzen March 1945
Cougino, Heinz	109565	Auschwitz, Malk Mathausen Apr 1945
Cougino, Helene	38911	Auschwitz, Ravensbruk, Malhof Apr 1945
Cougino, Salvator	109564	Auschwitz, Malk Mathausen Apr 1945
Cuenca, Anna	41732	Birkenau, Malhof July 1945
Cuenca, Charly	120846	Birkenau, Auschwitz, Warsaw, Dachau Apr 1945
Cuenca, Isaac	182484	Birkenau, Orienburg, Ordorf Apr 1945
Cuenca, Isac	120848	Birkenau, Auschwitz, Warsaw, Dachau Apr 1945
Daniel, Daniel	182543	Birkenau Jan 1945
Daniel, Solomon		Bergen Belsen Apr 1945
Eliakim, Solomon	116000	Auschwitz, Buna, Buchenwald Apr 1945
Eliaou, Benjamin	182044	Auschwitz, Zeuferzwamer, B Benza Apr 1945
Eliaou, Isac	182046	Auschwitz, Buna, Buchenwald Apr 1945
Eliaou, Rebecca	76877	Saltsweden Apr 1945
Errera, Joseph		Bergen Belsen Apr 1945

Errera, Linda		Bergen Belsen Apr 1945
Eskenazi, Moise	111260	Birkenau, Warsaw, Maldorf Apr 1945
Florentin, Dora	45023	Birkenau, Ravensbruk Apr 1945
Florentin, Liaou		Mueberg-Wienburg, Friesach Mark May 1945
Florentin, Oscar	120872	Birkenau, Yavozno, Buchenwald, Dachau May 1945
Florentin, Palomba	30239	Birkenau, Auschwitz, Ravensbruk May 1945
Florentin, Peppo	120873	Birkenau, Yavozno, Buchenwald, Dachau May 1945
Frances, Albert		Bergen Belsen Feb 1944
Frances, Sol		Bergen Belsen Feb 1944
Franco, Salomon	118621	Birkenau, Warsaw, Mildorf Apr 1945
Gattegno, Haim	112342	Birkenau, Dachau, Belsen Apr 1945
Gattegno, Louna	40077	Birkenau, Auschwitz, Bergen Belsen, April 1945
Gattegno, Rachel		Birkenau Jun 1945
Gattegno, Stella	39325	Birkenau, Auschwitz, Belsen Apr 1945
Gazes, Jeaques		Somovich, June 1945
Gazes, Sol 40006		Birkenau April 1945
Goldstein, Isaac	117286	Auschwitz, Mathauzen Apr 1945
Goldstein, Paul	117287	Auschwitz, Mauthauzen April 1945
Grotta, Estherina	41512	Birkenau, Auschwitz, Bergen Belsen Apr 1945
Guerchon, Eleanora		Birkenau, Revensbruk April 1945
Haguel, Leon	118633	Yawozno, Birkenau, Dlehanes, Jan 1945
Haguel, Solomon	124538	Birkenau, Warsaw, Dachau, May 1945
Halegua, Aron	115965	Auschwitz, Wasraw, Muldorf, Apr 1945
Halegua, Jacob	113108	Birkenau, Auchwitz May 1945
Halegua, Moise	137034	Birkenau, Warsaw, Dahau May 1945
Halegua, Regina	77155	Birkenau, Auchwitz Feb 1945
Halegua, Regina	40000	Birkenau, Ravensbruk May 1945
Halegua, Semtov	110928	Birkenau, Buchenwald Apr 1945
Hassid, Lazar		Buna, Auschwitz, Buchenwald May 1945
Hasson, Aron		Bergen Belzen, Trobitz, Luckar Apr 1945
Hasson, Isac		Bergen Belzen, Trobitz Apr 1945
Hasson, Joseph		Bergen Belzen, Trobitz, Luckar Apr 1945
Lacoma, Leon	114394	Birkenau, Warsaw, Waldlager March 1945
Levy, Alfonse		Bergen Belsen Apr 1945
Levy, Bella		Birkenau, Auschwitz, Rechlin, March 1945
Levy, David	116496	Auschwitz, Buna,Warthausen, Bergen Belsen Apr 45
Levy, Elvira	39169	Birkenau, Ravensbrook March 1945
Levy, Gabriel	114378	Birkenau, Auschwitz, Buna, Bergen Belsen Apr 1945
Levy, Leon	115122	Auschwitz, Buna, Buchenwald, Glaiwitz April 1945
Levy, Loutcha	40713	Birkenau, Neustadt Apr 1945
Levy, Rozi		Bergen Belsen Apr 1945
Levy, Semaya	119911	Auschwitz, Buna, Neustadt, Mathausen March 1945
Levy, Sol		Bergen Belsen, Apr 1945
Mair, Haim	118719	Auschwitz, Mathausen, Cusen, Sxoj 4, May 1945
Mair, Haim	118719	Birkenau, Auschwitz, Mathausen, Cusem May 1945
Mair, Yohana	109595	Auschwitz, Babitz, Buchenwald May 1945
Mallah, Sido	110242	Auschwitz, Yaurvozno, Bergen Belsen Mar 1945
Mallah, Sido	110242	Auschwitz, Yawozno, Bergen-Belsen May 1945
Maneta, Solomon		Auschwitz, Mathausen, Evensee May 1945

Mano, Avram	109612	Auschwitz, Birkenau, Buchenwald Apr 1945
Mano, Avram	109612	Auschwitz, Birkenau, Buchenwald April 1945
Mano, Benvenida	38861	Auschwitz, Neustadt, Aug 1945
Mano, Bienvenida	38861	Birkenau, Auschwitz, Neustadt Apr 1945
Mano, Solomon	118695	Birkenau, Orienburg, Landsberg May 1945
Masarano, Natan	182065	Auschwitz, Flassenburg, Dresden May 1945
Masarano, Natan	182065	Auschwitz, Flarosenburg, Dresden May 1945
Masarano, Sido	110259	Birkenau, Warsaw, Oberstradom Jan 1945
Maslia, Isac	119941	Auschwitz, Schwwtoblowitz, Mathausen May 1945
Massarano, Sido	110259	Birkenau, Varsovic, Oberstrandon Jan 1945
Matza, Rachel	76884	Auschwitz, Bergen Belsen April 1945
Menache, David		Bergen Belsen April 1945
Menache, Isac		Bergen Belsen April 1945
Menache, Marieta		Bergen Belsen April 1945
Menache, Ninia	40537	Birkenau, Auschwitz April 1945
Mesoulam, Sabetai	120979	Birkenau, Yawizno, Blehamer Feb 1945
Mesoulam, Sabetai	120979	Birkenau, Yavozno, Behamer Feb 1945
Mevorah, Bonika	76909	Auschwitz, Bergen Belsen April 1945
Mevorah, Menahem	182069	Auschwitz, Bina, Buchenwald April 1945
Mirada, Dario	115172	Auschwitz, Buna, Buchenwald, Dahau April 1945
Mirada, Sarina	76864	Birkenau, Bergen Belsen, Mathausen May 1945
Miranta, Dario	115172	Auschwitz, Buna, Buchenwald, Dachau Aug 1945
Mishahi, Juda		Belitgia, Sfetigratz May 1945
Mizan, Sabetai	116553	Auschwitz, Golechau April 1945
Molho, Annette	41098	Birkenau, Neustadt May 1945
Mordoh, Juda	114411	Birkenau, Auschwitz, Dahau May 1945
Mordoh, Stella	40566	Birkenau, Ravensbruk, Leipzig Aug 1945
Mordoh, Stella	40566	Birkenau, Ravemsbruk, Leipzig April 1945
Naar, Leon	115210	Auschwitz, Buna, Ausgburg, Dachau May 1945
Naar, Riqueta	40041	Birkenau, Newstadt May 1945
Nadjari, Avram	115216	Auschwitz, Buna, Bergen Belsen Apr 1945
Nadjari, Delicia	39631	Birkenau, Auschwitz, Bergen Belsen Apr 1945
Nadjari, Israel	115217	Auschwitz, Buchenwald Apr 1945
Nahmai, Mair	124476	Birkenau, Warsaw, Dachau, Waldlager May 1945
Nahmias, Sara	42893	Birkenau, Mialhof May 1945
Nahoumi, Gabriel	112518	Birkenau, Yawozin, Blehaner Feb 1945
Nahoumi, Haim	110309	Birkenau, Warsaw, Dublin April 1945
Nahoumi, Stella	76993	Birkenau, Bergen Belsen April 1945
Namias, Haim		Auschwitz, Melk., Ebensse May 1945
Nathan, Hazkia	115191	Auschwitz, Mauthauzen May 1945
Nathan, Joseph	137111	Birkenau, Warsaw May 1945
Nathan, Moise	121024	Auschwitz, Mauthauzen May 1945
Nissim, Alegre	76905	Birkenau, Bergen Belsen April 1945
Nissim, David	111370	Birkenau, Auchwitz, Warsaw Jun 1945
Ouziel, Solomon		Bergen Belsen Apr 1945
Pardo, Jacob	115246	Auschwitz, Buna, Flosenburg Mar 45
Parente, Isac	112535	Birkenau, Warsaw Apr 45
Parente, Isac	116575	Auschwitz, Warsaw, Dahau, Muldorf May 45
Parente, Rachel	77061	Birkenau, Bergen Belsen Apr 45

Pelosof, Dino		Mulberg, Sienburg Mar 45
Pesah, Daniel		Mausburg, Auscburg Apr 45
Pesah, Eliaou	122375	Birkenau, Yavozno, Warsaw, Dahau Mar 45
Pinhas, Daniel	115233	Auschwitz, Bergen Belsen Mar 45
Pitson, Alegre	76890	Birkenau, Bergen Belsen Apr 45
Pitson, Avram	121050	Birkenau, Buna, Auschwitz, Buhenvald Apr 45
Pitson, Dadi	117380	Auschwitz, Buna, Neustadt Mar 45
Pitson, Natan	115227	Auschwitz, Buna, Neustadt Mar 45
Profeta, Samuel	111383	Birkenau, Auschwitz May 45
Rumba, Derpoina	39310	Birkenau, Auschwitz, Ravensbruk May 1945
Saatzoglou, Anna	39405	Birkenau, Berjinke, Ravensbruk Sept 1945
Saia, Alegre	40595	Birkenau, Bergen Belsen Sept 1945
Saia, Esther	39292	Birkenau, Auschwitz, Neustadt, May 1945
Saia, Joseph	116257	Auschwitz, Budi, Dachau, Buchenwald Apr 1945
Saias, David	116256	Auschwitz, Buna, Warsaw, Dachau, Maldorf, Bavaria Aug 1945
Saias, Mair	116255	Auschwitz, Buna, Birkenau, Flosenburg, Pocking Sept 1945
Salem, Mordohai	13254	Birkenau, Auschwitz, Mathausen, Santoroz Mar 1945
Saltiel, Alice		Bergen Belsen Feb 1944
Saltiel, Bella		Bergen Belsen Feb 1944
Saltiel, Daniel		Bergen Belsen Feb 1944
Saltiel, Jacob	116605	Auschwitz, Buna, Apr 1945
Saltiel, Rene		Birkenau, Gilbert-Czechoslovakia
Saltiel, Salomon		
Saltiel, Sentov		Bergen Belsen Feb 1944
Saporta, Eliezer		Bergen Belsen Feb 1944
Saporta, Oro		Bergen Belsen Feb 1944
Sarfatti, Jeacque	137147	Birkenau, Warsaw, Logie Jun 1945
Sarfatti, Julie		Bergen Belsen Mar 1945
Sasson, David	116251	Auschwitz, Buna, Birkenau, Makimburg, Abbistate Sept 1945
Sasson, Gracia	44947	Birkenau, Waise-Wasser Mar 1945
Schiaky, Avram		Bergen Belsen Apr 1945
Schiaky, Reyna		Bergen Belsen Apr 1945
Schiaky, Solomon		Bergen Belsen Apr 1945
Schoulhami, Daisy	39168	Auschwitz, Birkenau, Malchau, May 5,1945
Seul, Emilie	46071	Auschwitz, Ravensbruk, Neustadt May 1945
Sevy, Baruh	115297	Auschwitz, Buna, Bergen Belsen May 1945
Sevy, Daniel	115298	Auschwitz, Buna, Firstegrauf, Bergen Belsen Sept 1945
Sevy, Isaac	137141	Birkenau, Warsaw, Valte-lager, Vilara Apr 1945
Sevy, Isac	115301	Auschwitz, Buna, Birkenau, Flosenburg, Leitmeritz Dec 1945
Sevy, Sadicario		
Sevy, Stella	44573	Birkenau, Weis-Wasser May 1945
Sevy, Sylvia	40167	Birkenau, Auschwitz, Malhof Mar 1945
Simha, Daniel	115315	Auschwitz, Buna, Mathausen Mar 1945
Sion, Buena		Bergen Belsen Apr 1945
Soustiel, Mathilde	40685	Birkenau, Weis-Waser June 1945
Tarfon, Aron	109774	Auschwitz, Budi, Buchenwald Aug 1945
Tarfon, Juda	116285	Auschwitz, Elenethohlowitz, Dachau May 1945
Tarfon, Solomon	116652	Auschwitz, Buna, Plathungen May 1945
Toppan, Isaac	118825	Birkenau, Vavozno, Warsaw, Dachau May 1945

Touvi, Isac	110476	Birkenau, Warsaw, Loblin May 1945
Vaena, Josua	109781	Auschwitz, Babrtez, Buna, May 1945
Vaena, Noemie	A8311	Birkenau Jan 1945
Varsano, Raphael	115365	Auschwitz, Mathauzen May 1945
Varsano, Salvator	118833	Birkenau, Auschwitz, Warsaw May 1945
Venezia, Clara	77037	Birkenau, Bergen Belsen May 1945
Wannung, Gilbert		Bergen Belsen Feb 1944
Wannung, Isac		Bergen Belsen Feb 1944
Wannung, May		Bergen Belsen Feb 1944
Wannung, Nissim		Bergen Belsen Feb 1944
Wannung, Rene		Bergen Belsen Feb 1944
Wannung, Stella		Bergen Belsen Feb 1944
Yehezkel, Baruch	110681	Birkenau, Lakija, Auschwitz, Mallhausen May 45
Yomtov, Albert	117299	Birkenau, Munich, May 1945
Yomtov, Jenny	39018	Birkenau, Auschwitz, Ravensbruk April 1945
Yomtov, Samuel	117300	Birkenau, Buna, Auschwitz, Buchenwald May 1945
Youchah, Martha	40760	Birkenau, Auschwitz, Ravensbrook, May 1945
Youchah, Samuel	137182	Birkenau, Warsaw, Dachau, Waldlager May 1945
Zaharia, Moise	182124	Auschwitz, Buna, Buchenwald Apr 1945

Appendix B

In 1955, The Greek newspaper, *ETHNOS*, published a series of articles by G. Sporides, entitled, "**The Great Persecution (The Decimation of Greek Jews)**". Since there were few photographs depicting many of the outrageous and despicable situations that the Nazis perpetrated on the Salonika Jewish community, the articles were accompanied by a series of illustrations based upon the testimony of those who suffered.

Semaya Abraham Levy collected the illustrations from this series and stored them in his archives.

Sampi Saltiel, President of the Israeli community in Thessaloniki with his head bent over, trembling and afraid, was standing in front of Dr. Kalmes waiting for his orders. Next to him, Zak Albala, interpreter, was also shaking because he faced the secret police's anger. Kalmes looked at them and his lips were full of rage.

The Great Persecution, January 18, 1955

They would load them on the trucks and send them out to break rocks, build roads for the German military machine. The Jews would arrive at the forced labor projects almost naked. Without a blanket or any other piece of clothing.
The Great Persecution, January 19, 1955

A crowd of scared people was gathered outside the three-story building of Jewish community and was trying to find out what was the hidden meaning behind the Gestapo's announcement concerning deportations to labor camps.
The Great Persecution, January 20, 1955

Rene Burkar, representative of the International Red Cross in Thessaloniki, appeared before the Commander of the Vehrmacht and complained about the martyrs and the humiliations done to the Jews at Victory Square. The German Commander listened to him, but he was clearly aggravated.
The Great Persecution, January 21, 1955

He still remembered all the torture. "Fall down" the order came in broken Greek. "Roll around in the mud ! " What could he do? He rolled...And heard laughter above him.
The Great Persecution, January 22, 1955

151

Under the burning sun that kills, the Jewish slaves are working on the scorched rocks of the Greek countryside. They break rocks and build railroads under the tough Nazi lash.
The Great Persecution, January 25, 1955

The Hitler whip was a daily occurance. For nothing, Israeli slaves would get whipped to death. In those sadistic penalties, all laborers of the camp would have to be present so that they would learn from beating.
The Great Persecution, January 26, 1955

The executions would take place suddenly. The condemned would be taken to the rocks and shot like dogs. A handkerchief over the eyes was the only human act of a Hitler.
The Great Persecution, January 27, 1955

One day a few laborers from a nearby camp who were sick but lucky enough to stumble upon an Austrian soldier and were not executed appeared. Their *condition and misery amazed people.*
The Great Persecution, January 28, 1955

The families of the slaves would sell whatever they owned just to send a piece of clothing, a package with food to their people who were suffering at force labor locations. Their pain was indescribable, all their belongings on the streets.
The Great Persecution, January 29, 1955

About the authors:

Semaya A. Levy was born in Thessaloniki, Greece, in 1913. He survived the Great Fire of 1917, occupation by the Nazis in 1941 and deportation to Auschwitz-Birkenau in 1943. He immigrated to Los Angeles, California in 1956, where he wrote this memoir about life in his beloved Salonika. He died on March 16, 1975, in Los Angeles. His daughter Rachel discovered her father's book, and has worked ceaselessly to have it published.

William A. Meis, Jr. is an editor, novelist, poet and publisher who has written numerous books, collaborated on many more, and publishes the **Fallen Bros Press** catalogue of fiction, essays and memoirs. He was the co-founder of the influential international journal, *New Perspectives Quarterly (NPQ)*, and a long-time Director of Publications for the Writers Guild of America (west). He holds an MFA degree from Goddard College, and lives with his wife and young son in Southern California.

www.ingramcontent.com/pod-product-compliance
Lightning Source LLC
Chambersburg PA
CBHW060433090426
42733CB00011B/2257